EXAMINING THE PRESIDENT'S CYBERSECURITY INFORMATION-SHARING PROPOSAL

HEARING

BEFORE THE

COMMITTEE ON HOMELAND SECURITY HOUSE OF REPRESENTATIVES

ONE HUNDRED FOURTEENTH CONGRESS

FIRST SESSION

FEBRUARY 25, 2015

Serial No. 114–4

Printed for the use of the Committee on Homeland Security

Available via the World Wide Web: http://www.gpo.gov/fdsys/

U.S. GOVERNMENT PUBLISHING OFFICE

94–108 PDF   WASHINGTON : 2015

For sale by the Superintendent of Documents, U.S. Government Publishing Office
Internet: bookstore.gpo.gov   Phone: toll free (866) 512–1800; DC area (202) 512–1800
Fax: (202) 512–2104   Mail: Stop IDCC, Washington, DC 20402–0001

COMMITTEE ON HOMELAND SECURITY

MICHAEL T. McCAUL, Texas, *Chairman*

LAMAR SMITH, Texas
PETER T. KING, New York
MIKE ROGERS, Alabama
CANDICE S. MILLER, Michigan, *Vice Chair*
JEFF DUNCAN, South Carolina
TOM MARINO, Pennsylvania
STEVEN M. PALAZZO, Mississippi
LOU BARLETTA, Pennsylvania
SCOTT PERRY, Pennsylvania
CURT CLAWSON, Florida
JOHN KATKO, New York
WILL HURD, Texas
EARL L. "BUDDY" CARTER, Georgia
MARK WALKER, North Carolina
BARRY LOUDERMILK, Georgia
MARTHA MCSALLY, Arizona
JOHN RATCLIFFE, Texas

BENNIE G. THOMPSON, Mississippi
LORETTA SANCHEZ, California
SHEILA JACKSON LEE, Texas
JAMES R. LANGEVIN, Rhode Island
BRIAN HIGGINS, New York
CEDRIC L. RICHMOND, Louisiana
WILLIAM R. KEATING, Massachusetts
DONALD M. PAYNE, JR., New Jersey
FILEMON VELA, Texas
BONNIE WATSON COLEMAN, New Jersey
KATHLEEN M. RICE, New York
NORMA J. TORRES, California

BRENDAN P. SHIELDS, *Staff Director*
JOAN V. O'HARA, *General Counsel*
MICHAEL S. TWINCHEK, *Chief Clerk*
I. LANIER AVANT, *Minority Staff Director*

CONTENTS

EXAMINING THE PRESIDENT'S CYBERSECURITY INFORMATION-SHARING PROPOSAL

Wednesday, February 25, 2015

U.S. House of Representatives,
Committee on Homeland Security,
Washington, DC.

The committee met, pursuant to call, at 12:04 p.m., in Room 311, Cannon House Office Building, Hon. Michael T. McCaul [Chairman of the committee] presiding.

Present: Representatives McCaul, Rogers, Barletta, Clawson, Katko, Hurd, Carter, Walker, Loudermilk, McSally, Ratcliffe, Thompson, Jackson Lee, Langevin, Richmond, Payne, Vela, Watson Coleman, and Torres.

Chairman McCAUL. The Committee on Homeland Security will come to order.

First of all, my apologies to the Members and the witnesses. I had a conflict with the—on the Foreign Affairs Committee with the Secretary of State on the authorized use of military force against ISIS, which I think is a very relevant issue to this committee, as well, in terms of dealing with the threat where it exists before it can come into the United States. Anyway, I just want to thank everybody for your patience.

I will give this opening statement. Been involved in this issue for quite some time. To Suzanne and Phyllis Schneck, thank you for being here, Dr. Fischer.

At the dawn of the digital age, our Nation saw endless opportunities to generate prosperity by expanding our networks and connecting to the world. But today, American prosperity depends as much on defending those networks as it does on expanding them. Every day, our country faces digital intrusions from criminals, activists, terrorists, and nation-states like Russia, China, and Iran. The impact of those intrusions are felt everywhere; from our National security secrets to the personal information of Americans.

We cannot tolerate acts of cyber vandalism, theft, or cyber warfare, especially when they put our Nation's critical infrastructure at risk and when they steal American intellectual property and innovations. Accordingly, our Government must play a leading role in combating threats in the digital domain.

It is clear that safeguarding American cyber space is one of the great National security challenges of our time. We are confronted almost daily with frightening new precedents, such as North Korea's act on Sony Pictures; a cowardly act meant to intimidate Americans and stifle freedom of expression. This attack came from

(1)

a nation-state using a digital bomb to target and destroy computer systems here in the United States.

Iranian-backed hackers also demonstrated this capability when they attacked Saudi Arabia's national oil company, Aramco, and destroyed 30,000 computers. Iran also targeted and continues to target major U.S. banks to shut down websites and restrict Americans' ability to access their bank accounts.

Imagine this type of attack on our gas pipelines or power grids in the northeast. Such assaults on our critical infrastructure could cripple our economy and weaken our ability to defend the United States. These scenarios sometimes sound alarmist. But we must take them seriously, as they grow more realistic every day. Our adversaries are hard at work developing and refining cyber attack capabilities, and they are using them to intimidate our Government and threaten our people in both times of peace and times of conflict.

But the threat extends beyond the industrial engines that drive our economies, to the homes of Americans themselves. Criminals and countries alike can use cyber attacks to raid Americans' saving accounts or steal their personal health records. The recent breach of health insurer Anthem illustrates the intrusiveness of these attacks. That assault alone exposed the personal information of up to 80 million people, including the names, birth dates, and Social Security numbers of tens of millions of children.

But this is just the latest in a long string of cyber breaches targeting private citizens, a list that includes breaches at Target, Neiman Marcus, Home Depot, and J.P. Morgan. Our adversaries are also seeking to steal secrets from our Government and our most innovative companies. We know that Chinese hackers, for instance, continue to breach Federal networks for the purpose of espionage and attack major U.S. businesses to give themselves a competitive edge in the global economy.

Make no mistake, these attacks are costing Americans their time, their money, and their jobs. General Keith Alexander described cyber espionage and the loss of American intellectual property as the greatest transfer of wealth in human history.

Sadly, our laws are not keeping up with the threat. For instance, fearing legal liability, many private companies choose not to disclose the threats they see on their own networks, leaving others vulnerable to the same intrusions. We cannot leave the American people and our businesses to fend for themselves. Now more than ever, Congress must take aggressive action.

This year I will lead a renewed effort to push cybersecurity legislation through Congress. Last year, the Ranking Member and I in this committee passed five cybersecurity bills. These new statutes lay out the rules of the road on how cyber information will be shared between Government and the private sector so that the two can work together to combat this persistent threat.

The laws also provide important protections to ensure Americans' information and civil liabilities are not compromised. But now we must build on that success. We can start by creating a safe harbor, where legal barriers to share cyber threat information are removed and the private sector is encouraged to collaborate. This will allow us to respond to cyber incidents more quickly and effectively and will give Government and private entities the ability to see the threat landscape in real time.

I am pleased the President has come forward with a proposal on this important issue. Our solutions must transcend partisan boundaries if we are going to tackle this challenge, and the American people are counting on us.

Again, I want to thank the witnesses. I want to thank the Members for their patience here today.

[The statement of Chairman McCaul follows:]

STATEMENT OF CHAIRMAN MICHAEL T. MCCAUL

FEBRUARY 25, 2015

At the dawn of the digital age, our Nation saw endless opportunities to generate prosperity by expanding our networks and connecting to the world. But today, American prosperity depends as much on defending those networks as it does on expanding them.

Every day our country faces digital intrusions from criminals, hacktivists, terrorists, and nation-states like Russia, China, and Iran. The impacts of those intrusions are felt everywhere—from our National security secrets to the personal information of Americans.

We cannot tolerate acts of cyber vandalism, cyber theft, and cyber warfare especially when they put our Nation's critical infrastructure at risk and when they steal American intellectual property and innovation. Accordingly, our Government must play a leading role in combating threats in the digital domain.

It is clear that safeguarding American cyber space is one of the great National security challenges of our time. We are confronted almost daily with frightening new precedents, such as the North Korean cyber attack on Sony Pictures—a cowardly act meant to intimidate Americans and stifle freedom of expression.

This attack came from a nation-state using a digital bomb to target and destroy computer systems here in the United States. Iranian-backed hackers also demonstrated this capability when they attacked Saudi Arabia's national oil company, Aramco, and destroyed 30,000 computers. Iran also continues to target major U.S. banks to shut down websites and restrict Americans ability to access their bank accounts.

Imagine this type of attack on our gas pipelines or power grid in the Northeast. Such assaults on our critical infrastructure could cripple our economy and weaken our ability to defend the United States. These scenarios sometimes sound alarmist, but we must take them seriously as they grow more realistic every day. Our adversaries are hard at work developing and refining cyber attack capabilities, and they are using them to intimidate our Government and threaten our people in both times of peace and times of conflict.

But the threat extends beyond the industrial engines that drive our economy to the homes of Americans themselves. Criminals and countries alike can use cyber attacks to raid Americans' savings accounts or steal their personal health records.

The recent breach of health insurer, Anthem, illustrates the intrusiveness of these attacks. That assault alone exposed the personal information of up to 80 million people, including the names, birth dates, and social security numbers of tens of millions of children. But this is just the latest in a long string of cyber breaches targeting private citizens—a list that includes breaches at Target, Neiman Marcus, Home Depot, and JP Morgan.

Our adversaries are also seeking to steal secrets from our Government and our most innovative companies. We know that Chinese hackers, for instance, continue to breach Federal networks for the purpose of espionage and attack major U.S. businesses to give themselves a competitive edge in the global economy. Make no mistake: These attacks are costing Americans their time, money, and jobs. General Keith Alexander has described cyber espionage and the loss of American intellectual property as the "greatest transfer of wealth in history."

Sadly, our laws are not keeping up with the threat. For instance, fearing legal liability, many private companies choose to not disclose the threats they see on their own networks, leaving others vulnerable to the same intrusions.

We cannot leave the American people and our businesses to fend for themselves. Now, more than ever, Congress must take aggressive action.

This year I will lead a renewed effort to push cybersecurity legislation through Congress. Last year, the Ranking Member and I, and this committee, passed five

4

cyber bills. These new statutes lay out the rules of the road on how cyber information will be shared between Government and the private sector so that the two can work together to combat this persistent threat. The laws also provide important protections to ensure Americans' information and civil liberties are not compromised.

But now, we must build on that success. And, we can start by creating a "safe harbor" where legal barriers to sharing cyber threat information are removed and the private sector is encouraged to collaborate. This will allow us to respond to cyber incidents more quickly and effectively—and will give Government and private entities the ability to see the threat landscape in real time.

I am pleased the President has come forward with a proposal on this important issue. Our solutions must transcend partisan boundaries if we are going to tackle this challenge. The American people are counting on us.

I want to thank the witnesses for testifying before this committee and I look forward to your testimony.

Chairman MCCAUL. I now recognize the Ranking Member.

Mr. THOMPSON. Thank you very much, Mr. Chairman. Let me also welcome our witnesses and thank them for their patience on getting started.

Earlier, some of us were briefed on some on-going efforts by the Department, Mr. Chairman. I might add, it was very informative. Thank you all very much for doing it.

Our hearing today is examining the President's cybersecurity information-sharing proposal. Mr. Chairman, at its core cybersecurity relies on effective information sharing among network operators about indicator, hacks, and cyber vulnerabilities.

This committee has been central in its effort to foster better cyber information sharing by producing bipartisan cybersecurity legislation that President Obama signed into law at the end of last year. As you talked about it, the National Cybersecurity Protection Act of 2014 authorizes the National Cyber and Communications Integrity Center, NCCIC, within the Department of Homeland Security as an information-sharing hub for cybersecurity risk and incidents, and erected the NCCIC to provide technical assistance, risk management support, and incident response capabilities to impacted network operators.

The legislative proposal that the President unveiled last month has again spurred debate. Importantly, the administration's proposal would require participating companies to comply with certain privacy restrictions, such as removing unnecessary personal information and taking measures to protect any personal information to quality for liability protection. In my view, the President's proposal has some merit.

As we go forward, we should consider the following questions: First, what is being shared? Is it just computer code made up of zeros and ones, or does the information contain Americans' sensitive personal data? If it does contain personal data, I believe that reasonable efforts should be made by participating companies to remove personally identifiable information from the information shared with the Government that will help to preserve Americans' privacy.

Second, who is doing the sharing? Is it a critical infrastructure operator?

Third, where is the sharing happening? The answer to the question has privacy implications, particularly when the sharing is between the Federal Government and the private sector, as opposed to sharing between private-sector companies.

I look forward to hearing testimony from our witnesses on the
potential risks and rewards of a cyber information-sharing environment dominated by ISAO, as the President envisions. Certainly, I
would like to hear how the proposed changes could impact NCCIC.
The success of NCCIC is dependent on the companies' seeing the
value of proposition for sharing with the Department.

I look forward to hearing from the Department on how they intend to drive traffic to the NCCIC and how implementation of a
new cyber law is progressing. I would also like to hear more about
the new education grant program that the President has proposed.

While I am pleased that the President seems to agree about the
importance of making this investment in growing our cyber workforce, I am disappointed that the proposal calls for just $5 million
a year to be spent over 5 years at 13 historically black colleges and
universities and two National laboratories is disappointing, especially in light of a documented shortfall in cyber workforce. Given
the billions of dollars spent on cybersecurity, much of which is
spent on Federal contractors, I would have expected a more ambitious plan for developing cyber tactics.

Before I close, I would like to note that on February 11, together
with the Chairman and the leadership of its Senate Homeland Security and Governmental Affairs Committee, we wrote to the President about the new Cyber Threat Intelligence Integration Center.
We look forward to a formal response to our questions, particularly
as they relate to the NCCIC.

I look forward to hearing from our witnesses today and working
with the Chairman on forthcoming legislation to help ensure that
the networks of our Nation's critical infrastructure are more secure.

With that, I yield back.

[The statement of Ranking Member Thompson follows:]

STATEMENT OF RANKING MEMBER BENNIE G. THOMPSON

FEBRUARY 25, 2015

Over the past decade, we have witnessed an explosion of internet use in all aspects of life. As a Nation, we do more business on-line than ever before—trillions
of dollars a year. For most Americans, smartphones, tablets, and other computers
have become the platforms on which we live, work, and play.

Unfortunately, these devices and networks have also become targets for bad actors.

Last month's cyber attack on the Nation's second-largest health insurer, Anthem,
resulted in tens of millions of Social Security numbers, birth dates, addresses, and
names being stolen from its database. Given that Anthem insures 7.5 million people
in 14 States, the potential damage of this breach is expected to be extensive.

Last year's attack on Sony destroyed data, disabled thousands of computers, and
exposed the personal information of Sony employees.

These attacks underscore that any network that is connected to the internet is
a potential victim.

The fact that our Nation's critical infrastructure—including the power grid, financial institutions, and health care systems—are all connected to the internet make
them particularly attractive targets for attack.

Cyber attackers are constantly probing for weaknesses in our critical infrastructure which powers much of our electric grid, financial institutions, and health care
systems.

The attention that cybersecurity has received in recent years by President Obama
and Congress is reflective of the increasing awareness that the responsibility to address this homeland security threat is a collective one.

At its core, cybersecurity relies on effective information sharing among network operators about indicators, hacks, and cyber vulnerabilities.

This committee has been central in efforts to foster better cyber information sharing by producing bipartisan cybersecurity legislation that President Obama signed into law at the end of last year.

The "National Cybersecurity Protection Act of 2014" authorizes the National Cybersecurity and Communications Integrity Center (NCCIC) within the Department of Homeland Security as an information-sharing hub for cybersecurity risks and incidents, and directed the NCCIC to provide technical assistance, risk management support, and incident response capabilities to impacted network operators.

The legislative proposal that the President unveiled last month has, again, spurred debate.

Importantly, the administration's proposal would require participating companies to comply with certain privacy restrictions such as removing unnecessary personal information and taking measures to protect any personal information to qualify for liability protection.

In my view, the President's proposal has some merit.

As we go forward, we should consider the following questions: First, what is being shared?—Is it just computer code made up of "zeroes and ones" or does the information contain Americans' sensitive personal data? If it does contain personal data, I believe that "reasonable efforts" should be made by participating companies to remove "personally identifiable information" from information shared with the Government. This will help to preserve Americans' privacy.

Second, who is doing the sharing?—Is it a critical infrastructure operator?

Third, where is the sharing happening?—The answer to that question has privacy implications—particularly when the sharing is between the Federal Government and the private sector, as opposed to sharing between private-sector companies.

I look forward to hearing testimony from our witnesses on the potential risks and rewards of a cyber information-sharing environment dominated by ISAOs, as the President envisions.

Certainly, I would like to hear how these proposed changes could impact the NCCIC. The success of the NCCIC is dependent on companies seeing the "value proposition" for sharing with the Department.

I look forward to hearing from the Department on how they intend to drive traffic to the NCCIC and how implementation of the new cyber law is progressing.

I would also like to hear more about the new education grant program that the President has proposed.

While I am pleased that the President seems to agree about the importance of making this investment in growing our cyber workforce, I am disappointed that the proposal calls for just $5 million a year to be spent over 5 years at 13 Historically Black Colleges and Universities, and two National laboratories, is disappointing.

Given the billions of dollars spent on cybersecurity, much of which is spent on Federal contractors, I would have expected a more ambitious plan for developing cyber talent.

Before I close, I would like to acknowledge that the committee just met with the President's cybersecurity advisor, Michael Daniel. I appreciate Mr. Daniel's willingness to lay out the administration's vision for cybersecurity and to address our questions, particularly about the newly-announced cyber center that will be housed in the intelligence community.

On February 11, together with the Chairman and the leadership of the Senate Homeland Security and Governmental Affairs Committee, we wrote to the President about this new "Cyber Threat Intelligence Integration Center". We look forward to a formal response to our questions, particularly as they relate to the NCCIC.

In conclusion, I look forward to hearing from our witnesses today and to working with the Chairman on forthcoming legislation to help ensure that the networks of our Nation's critical infrastructure are more secure.

Chairman MCCAUL. Thank the Ranking Member.

Chairman now recognizes the—I would like to briefly introduce the witnesses. First, we have the Honorable Suzanne Spaulding. She is the under secretary for the National Protection and Programs Directorate at the Department of Homeland Security.

Next, we have Dr. Phyllis Schneck. She is a deputy under secretary for cybersecurity and communications within the National Protection and Programs Directorate at the Department of Homeland Security. It is great to have both of you here today.

Finally, we have Dr. Eric Fischer, who is a senior specialist for science and technology at the Congressional Research Service.

The witnesses' full statements will appear in the record. The Chairman now recognizes Ms. Spaulding for 5 minutes.

STATEMENT OF SUZANNE E. SPAULDING, UNDER SECRETARY, NATIONAL PROTECTION AND PROGRAMS DIRECTORATE, U.S. DEPARTMENT OF HOMELAND SECURITY

Ms. SPAULDING. Thank you, Chairman McCaul, Ranking Member Thompson, Members of the committee.

We are very pleased to be here today to discuss the administration's proposal to enhance cybersecurity information sharing. This proposal recognizes the unique mission and capabilities of the Department of Homeland Security's National Protection and Programs Directorate. It will facilitate information sharing in ways that will significantly advance our National security.

By placing the Department's National Cybersecurity and Communications Integration Center, or NCCIC, as the coordination center for receiving and disseminating cyber threat indicator information, which will be very quickly shared. We will receive and disseminate that information to Federal and non-Federal entities.

As this committee knows, we are faced with pervasive cyber threats from a variety of actors, including nation-state actors. They are motivated by a range of objectives, including espionage, political and ideological beliefs, and financial gain.

The National Preparedness and Protection Directorate focuses on helping our partners across Government and non-Government to manage those cyber risks, to reduce the frequency and impact of cyber incidents, and to build their own capacity. We do this by sharing timely and accurate information and analysis, particularly to enable the private and public-sector partners to protect themselves. This includes detailed analysis about cascading consequences in the physical world that can result from cyber incidents.

We provide technology to detect and block cyber threats from impacting the dot.gov networks, the civilian Government networks, and enable those agencies to more readily identify network security issues and prioritize the actions that they must take to address those.

We enable commercial cybersecurity companies to use Government-furnished Classified information to better protect their private-sector customers. We provide on-site assistance to critical infrastructure and Federal agencies who have been impacted by a significant cyber incident. We maintain a trusted environment for private-sector partners to share information and to collaborate to address cybersecurity threats and trends.

Congress' support for these activities led to the bipartisan action last year to pass critical cybersecurity legislation. That legislation enhanced our ability to work with the private sector and with other Federal civilian departments. As been noted, it strengthened the Department's ability to recruit and to retain the kind of cybersecurity exerts that we now have on-board.

Enactment of these bills represents significant progress in the Department's cybersecurity mission. I am very grateful to Congress, to this committee, and particularly to Chairman McCaul and Ranking Member Thompson, who contributed significant efforts to ensure the enactment of this legislation.

But we need to keep moving forward. Additional legislation is needed. Carefully updating laws to facilitate cybersecurity information sharing is essential to improving the Nation's cybersecurity. While many companies currently do share cybersecurity information with each other and with the Government under existing laws, there is a growing need to increase the volume and the speed of such information sharing, without sacrificing the trust of the American people or individual privacy and civil liberties.

The President's legislative proposal incentivizes private entities to share information with the Government through that National Cybersecurity and Integration Center, or NCCIC, that I mentioned earlier. That is our 24/7 operations and watch center. It brings together currently Government partners from across the Government and the private sector. This is important.

The NCCIC's core mission, as stated in this committee's unanimously-passed National Cybersecurity Protection Act, is coordinating and serving as the interface for cybersecurity information across the Government and the private sector. We do this with strong protections in place for protecting privacy and for protecting sensitive business information.

Having a single designated entry point into the Government makes it easier to ensure that privacy protections are being consistently applied across the Government. It reduces the complexity for the private sector that wonders where to go. It improves our ability to develop a common operating picture of the cyber threats that we see daily. It helps us to connect the dots, if you will, with regard to cyber threats.

I understand that Chairman McCaul has invited Members of this committee to visit and tour our National Cybersecurity Communications Integration Center. I look forward to seeing many of you there and continuing this discussion at that time.

Before I close, I would like to reiterate Secretary Johnson's comments on the Department's funding situation. Congress still has not passed a fiscal year 2015 appropriations bill for the Department of Homeland Security. As long as we operate on a continuing resolution, we are hampered by uncertainty and the inability to fund vital new homeland security initiatives. Without funding, NPBD's cybersecurity and critical infrastructure mission will be significantly impacted.

Let me end by saying that today, our adversaries can exploit a fundamental asymmetry in our network infrastructure. While nearly all of our systems and networks are globally interconnected, our defensive capabilities are not yet. This gives the attacker a compelling advantage. They can find and exploit weak links in our systems from anywhere around the world at machine speed. By sharing cyber threat indicators in near real time, we can and will reduce that asymmetry.

I want to thank you for this opportunity to testify. I look forward to your questions.

I turn it over to my cyber deputy, Dr. Phyllis Schneck.

[The joint prepared statement of Ms. Spaulding and Ms. Schneck follows:]

JOINT PREPARED STATEMENT OF SUZANNE E. SPAULDING AND PHYLLIS SCHNECK

FEBRUARY 25, 2015

INTRODUCTION

Chairman McCaul, Ranking Member Thompson, and distinguished Members of the committee, we are pleased to appear today to discuss the President's cybersecurity legislative proposal on information sharing.

In our testimony today, we will highlight the Department of Homeland Security (DHS) National Protection and Programs Directorate cybersecurity role and capabilities, and describe how the President's legislative proposal to facilitate cyber threat indicator information sharing will further our National security, with DHS's National Cybersecurity and Communications Integration Center (NCCIC) as the coordination center to receive and disclose cyber threat indicators to Federal and Non-Federal entities.

THE ON-GOING CYBER THREAT AND THE DHS CYBERSECURITY ROLE

As a Nation, we are faced with pervasive cyber threats. Malicious actors, including those at nation-state level, are motivated by a variety of reasons that include espionage, political and ideological beliefs, and financial gain. Increasingly, State, Local, Tribal and Territorial (SLTT) networks are experiencing cyber activity of a sophistication level similar to that seen on Federal networks.

To achieve our cybersecurity mission, the National Protection and Programs Directorate focuses on helping our partners understand and manage cyber risk, reduce the frequency and impact of cyber incidents, and build partner capacity. We share timely and accurate information and analysis to enable private and public-sector partners to protect themselves. We provide on-site assistance to Federal agencies and critical infrastructure entities impacted by a significant cybersecurity incident. We provide technology and services to detect and block cyber threats from impacting Federal civilian networks. We enable Federal agencies to more readily identify network security issues and take prioritized action. We enable commercial cybersecurity companies to use Classified information so they can better protect their private-sector customers. We perform comprehensive consequence analyses that assess cross-sector interdependencies and cascading effects, including the potential for kinetic harm that includes loss of life, and we maintain a trusted environment for private-sector partners to share information and collaborate on cybersecurity threats and trends.

DHS's National Cybersecurity and Communications Integration Center

The NCCIC serves as a 24x7 centralized location for the coordination and integration of cyber situational awareness and incident management. NCCIC partners include all Federal departments and agencies; State, local, Tribal, and territorial governments; the private sector; and international entities. The NCCIC continues to explore opportunities to expand its liaison capacity from other agencies and the private sector. The NCCIC provides its partners with enhanced situational awareness of cybersecurity and communications incidents and risks, and provides timely information to manage vulnerabilities, threats, and incidents. In 2014, the NCCIC received over 97,000 incident reports, and issued nearly 12,000 actionable cyber alerts or warnings. NCCIC teams also detected over 64,000 significant vulnerabilities on Federal and non-Federal systems and directly responded to 115 significant cyber incidents.

The NCCIC actively shares cyber threat indicators to and from multiple sources including private-sector partners, the intelligence community, Federal Departments and agencies, law enforcement, State, local, Tribal, and territorial governments, and international governments. This sharing, which has been taking place for many years, takes many forms including person-to-person interactions on the NCCIC floor, manual exchange of information via e-mail and secure web portals, and more recently via automated, machine-to-machine exchanges in STIX and TAXII protocols. While all of these sharing methods have value, the cybersecurity community has recognized the strategic importance of migrating cyber threat indicator sharing to more automated mechanisms when and where appropriate.

CYBERSECURITY LEGISLATION

Last year, Congress acted in a bipartisan manner to pass critical cybersecurity legislation that enhanced the ability of the Department of Homeland Security to work with the private sector and other Federal civilian departments in each of their own cybersecurity activities, and enhanced the Department's cyber workforce authorities. Enactment of these bills represents a significant moment for the Department's cybersecurity mission, and this committee in particular undertook significant efforts to bring the bills to passage. We are thankful for your support and we are deploying those additional authorities with clarity of mission.

Additional legislation is needed. We must take additional steps to ensure that DHS is able to rapidly and efficiently deploy new protective technologies across Federal civilian agency information systems. In addition, carefully updating laws to facilitate cybersecurity information sharing within the private sector and between the private and Government sectors is also essential to improving the Nation's cybersecurity. While many companies currently share cybersecurity threat information under existing laws, there is a heightening need to increase the volume and speed of information shared without sacrificing the trust of the American people or the protection of privacy, confidentiality, civil rights, or civil liberties. It is essential to ensure that cyber threat information can be shared quickly among trusted partners, including with law enforcement, so that network owners and operators can take necessary steps to block threats and avoid damage.

The NCCIC plays a critical role in the President's recent legislative proposal because its core mission—as articulated in the National Cybersecurity Protection Act, developed by this committee and unanimously passed by the House in December—is to coordinate and serve as an interface for cybersecurity information across the Government and private sector.

The Administration's Information-Sharing Proposal for Cyber Threat Indicators

Building on the bipartisan cybersecurity legislation enacted last Congress, President Obama visited the NCCIC on January 13, 2015, to announce a proposal for additional legislation to improve cybersecurity information sharing. The President noted, "Much of our critical infrastructure runs on networks connected to the Internet . . . [a]nd most of this infrastructure is owned and operated by the private sector. So neither Government nor the private sector can defend the Nation alone. It's going to have to be a shared mission—Government and industry working hand in hand, as partners." This partnership entails sharing cyber threat indicators to better enable Government agencies and the private sector to protect themselves.

Information sharing, especially of these technical "threat indicators" that can be used to identify and block malicious activity, is the lifeblood of effective cyber defense and response. Pulling together this information allows defenders to identify anomalies or patterns and recognize dangerous activity before it can do significant damage. The goal of the President's proposal is to increase the sharing of this type of information, as quickly as possible, with appropriate protection for privacy and of sensitive information and systems.

Among other things, the administration's proposal would reduce the risks for private entities to voluntarily share technical cyber threat indicators with each other and the NCCIC by providing protections against civil or criminal liability for such sharing. Equally important, the proposal narrowly defines the threat indicators that will be shared, requires that irrelevant identifying information be minimized from these indicators, and generally requires strong protections for the privacy and confidentiality of personal information. Finally, the proposal calls for the creation of Information Sharing and Analysis Organizations (ISAOs). ISAOs would be information sharing organizations that would help speed information sharing within the private sector and between the private sector and Government.

Our goal is to expand information sharing within the private sector, and to build on the existing relationships, processes and programs of the NCCIC to enhance cooperation between the Government and private sector. The proposal will help us improve the methods that the NCCIC already uses to share cyber threat indicators, and leverage automation to achieve scalability wherever possible. We look to evolve and expand indicator sharing at the NCCIC from human exchanges, portals, and written reports to automated machine-to-machine communications. Our vision is that this may reduce the time to receive and act on indicators from hours to milliseconds, create consistency in information provided to interagency partners, law enforcement, and the private sector, and free analysts to focus on the threats that require human analysis while expediting detection and blocking of new threats.

NCCIC as the Coordination Center

Cyber threat indicators, which allow Government agencies and the private sector to better protect themselves, come from a variety of sources, including: Government agencies, private companies, international partners, and ISAOs. Given the variety of formats used—and information that is included—when sharing such information, the Government must have a central clearinghouse to ensure that privacy and confidentiality protections are consistently applied and that the right information reaches the right Government and private-sector entities.

DHS is a leader within the Government when it comes to the development and operational implementation of privacy, confidentiality, and civil liberties policies. DHS was the first agency to have statutorily established Officers for Privacy and for Civil Rights and Civil Liberties. From its creation, DHS has built both privacy and civil liberties protections into all of its programs and has dedicated, on-site privacy professionals committed to ensuring that its cyber mission is carried out in a way consistent with our Nation's values. Through statutory protections like Protected Critical Infrastructure Information (PCII), DHS will continue to anonymize the identity of submitters and other proprietary and sensitive information in threat indicator submissions. Moreover, the President's proposal calls for DHS to build upon its existing privacy, confidentiality, and civil liberty procedures by working with the Attorney General to develop new procedures to appropriately limit Government receipt, use, and retention of threat indicators. Establishing the NCCIC as the primary entry way for cyber threat indicators from the private sector will ensure uniform application of these important privacy and confidentiality protections, while still allowing cyber threat indictors to be shared with law enforcement for the specific purposes identified in the legislation.

NCCIC sits at the intersection of cyber communities, with representatives from the private sector and other Government entities physically present on the NCCIC floor and connected virtually. This diverse participation in the NCCIC was cemented by section 226(d) of the Homeland Security Act as added by the National Cybersecurity Protection Act. NCCIC's core mission is to enable better network defense by assessing and appropriately sharing information on the risks to America's critical cyber systems and how to reduce them.

BUILDING CAPACITY TO ACCELERATE AUTOMATED SHARING OF CYBER THREAT INDICATORS

The administration's proposal directs DHS to automate and share information in as close to real time as practicable with relevant Federal agencies, including law enforcement entities, and with ISAOs. For the past 3 years, DHS has led the development in collaboration with the private sector of specifications—known as STIX and TAXII—which standardize the representation and exchange of cyber threat information, including actionable cyber threat indicators. STIX, the Structured Threat Information eXpression, is a standardized format for the representation and exchange of cyber threat information, including indicators. TAXII, the Trusted Automated eXchange of Indicator Information, is a standardized protocol for discovering and exchanging cyber threat information in STIX. The interagency Enhance Shared Situational Awareness initiative has already chosen STIX as the basis for sharing cyber threat indicators between the Federal cyber centers, ensuring interoperability between these key sources of information.

Through collaboration between DHS and the private sector, there is a solid and rapidly-growing base of commercial offerings supporting STIX and sharing indicators via the TAXII, including platforms, network protection appliances and endpoint security tools. While the NCCIC has in-house systems and tools to assist analysts in generating STIX indicators, those indicators are currently analyzed and filtered by human analysts and shared back out with the private sector and Federal partners through manual methods such as e-mail and secure portals. In 2014, the NCCIC began a limited pilot with several organizations to test automated delivery of STIX indicators via TAXII.

To inform our plan for achieving automated cyber threat indicator information sharing, DHS created a working group between a range of DHS offices and the FBI, a critical stakeholder in the NCCIC. We also included experts from our Privacy, Civil Rights and Civil Liberties, and Science and Technology offices, among others, to ensure that our architecture is based on best-in-class technology and is consistent with our values and our respect for Americans' privacy and civil liberties.

Implementation will proceed through four major phases: (1) An initial operating capability phase in which we will deploy a TAXII system that can disseminate STIX cyber threat indicators with increased automation capability, enabling the use of human analysis for the most complex problems and egregious threats; (2) an expanded automation phase in which we will develop and deploy DHS infrastructure that can receive, filter, and analyze cyber threat indicators—during this phase, we will promulgate guidance for private-sector companies to minimize, redact, and tag their data prior to submission to NCCIC, and will complete a Privacy Impact Assessment; (3) a final operating capability phase in which we will fully automate DHS processes to receive and appropriately disseminate cyber threat indicators in a machine-readable format and finalize policies for filtering, receipt, retention, use, and sharing, including regular compliance reviews; and (4) a scaled services capability phase, during which DHS will work to enable agencies that lack sufficient cybersecurity resources or expertise to receive and share cyber threat indicators with the NCCIC in near-real time by providing a turnkey technical solution to "plug in" to the NCCIC.

DHS SHARES INFORMATION WIDELY WITH FEDERAL AGENCIES AND THE PRIVATE SECTOR

Currently, DHS shares information with Federal agencies and the private sector. DHS takes a customer-focused approach to information sharing, and different types of information require differing response times and dissemination protocols. DHS provides information to detect and block cybersecurity attacks on Federal civilian agencies and shares information to help critical infrastructure entities in their own protection; provides information to commercial cybersecurity companies so they can better protect their customers through the Enhanced Cybersecurity Services program, or ECS; and maintains a trusted information-sharing environment for private-sector partners to share information and collaborate on cybersecurity threats and trends via a program known as the Cyber Information Sharing and Collaboration Program, or CISCP. This trust derives in large part from our emphasis on privacy, confidentiality, civil rights, and civil liberties across all information-sharing programs, including special care to safeguard personally identifiable information.

DHS also directly supports Federal civilian departments and agencies in developing capabilities that will improve their own cybersecurity posture. Through the Continuous Diagnostics and Mitigation (CDM) program, DHS enables Federal agencies to more readily identify network security issues, including unauthorized and unmanaged hardware and software; known vulnerabilities; weak configuration settings; and potential insider attacks. Agencies can then prioritize mitigation of these issues based upon potential consequences or likelihood of exploitation by adversaries. The CDM program provides diagnostic sensors, tools, and dashboards that provide situational awareness to individual agencies, and will provide DHS with summary data to understand relative and system risk across the Executive branch. DHS is moving aggressively to implement CDM across all Federal civilian agencies, and Memoranda of Agreement with the CDM program encompass over 97 percent of all Federal civilian personnel.

While CDM will identify vulnerabilities and systemic risks within agency networks, the National Cybersecurity Protection System, also known as EINSTEIN, detects and blocks threats at the perimeter of those networks or at an agencies' Internet Service Provider. EINSTEIN is an integrated intrusion detection, analysis, information-sharing, and intrusion-prevention system. The most recent iteration, Einstein 3 Accelerated (E3A), supplements EINSTEIN 2 by adding additional intrusion prevention capabilities and enabling Internet Service Providers (ISPs), under the direction of DHS, to detect and block known or suspected cyber threats using indicators.

CONCLUSION

We are working together to find new and better ways to share accurate, timely data in a manner consistent with fundamental American values of privacy, confidentiality, and civil rights. While securing cyberspace has been identified as a core DHS mission since the 2010 Quadrennial Homeland Security Review, the Department's view of cybersecurity has evolved to include a more holistic emphasis on critical infrastructure which takes into account the convergence of cyber and physical risk.

Today our adversaries exploit a fundamental asymmetry in our network infrastructure: While nearly all of our systems and networks are globally interconnected, our defensive capabilities are not. This gives the attackers a compelling advantage as they can find and exploit the weak links in our systems from anywhere around the world—at machine speed. By sharing cyber threat indicators in near-real time, we reduce that asymmetry.

As our defensive cybersecurity capabilities become more interconnected, we greatly reduce the likelihood that an adversary can re-use attack infrastructure, tools, tactics, techniques, and procedures. In addition, we greatly reduce the time window in which new and novel attacks are effective because the ecosystem shares those indicators and develops a type of "herd immunity," improving defenses as indicators are shared and events are correlated in near-real time. These two factors do not eliminate all cyber threats, but they hold the promise of significantly increasing the time and resources (both technical and human) that attackers must expend to achieve their goals. Moreover, the STIX data format and the TAXII transport method are increasingly compatible with commonly-used commercial information technology (IT) products. This means more entities are able to send indicators automatically to the NCCIC, creating an ecosystem of indicators which will in turn provide greater context to malicious cyber activity and rapidly increase situational awareness per Executive Order 13636, *Improving Critical Infrastructure Cybersecurity* and Executive Order 13691, signed February 13, 2015, *Promoting Private Sector Cybersecurity Information Sharing.*

DHS will continue to serve as one of the Government's primary resources for information sharing and collaborative analysis, at machine speed wherever possible, of global cyber risks, trends, and incidents. Through our leadership role in protecting civilian Government systems and helping the private sector protect itself, DHS can correlate data from diverse sources, in an anonymized and secure manner, to maximize insights and inform effective risk mitigation.

DHS provides the foundation of the U.S. Government's approach to securing and ensuring the resilience of civilian critical infrastructure and essential services. We look forward to continuing the conversation and supporting the American goals of peace and stability; in these endeavors, we rely upon your continued support.

Thank you for the opportunity to testify, and we look forward to any questions you may have.

Chairman MCCAUL. Thank you, Ms. Spaulding. We appreciate your service and dedication to this important issue.

The Chairman now recognizes Dr. Schneck.

STATEMENT OF PHYLLIS SCHNECK, DEPUTY UNDER SECRETARY, CYBERSECURITY AND COMMUNICATIONS, NATIONAL PROTECTION AND PROGRAMS DIRECTORATE, U.S. DEPARTMENT OF HOMELAND SECURITY

Ms. SCHNECK. Good morning and thank you Chairman McCaul, Ranking Member Thompson, and distinguished Members of the committee.

Let me echo Under Secretary Spaulding's thanks for convening this meeting today. Thank you for your tireless support to our cyber mission and thank you for making it a constant between my time in the private sector and my time now in Government, the impact that our work and our legislative process can have on good things.

The under secretary explained the Department of Homeland Security's role and capabilities in cybersecurity and explained why our National Cybersecurity and Communications Integration Center, our NCCIC, is key and at the forefront of the President's proposal for increasing the volume and speed of information sharing.

I would like to amplify that and tell you how we are going to do this and how we are building that capability. First, to the Ranking Member's question; what is being shared and what do we need most? We need information sharing and especially the technical threat indicators; the bare bones information of, for example, what is an address of a machine that is doing something bad that we see? What is the specific code of software that is being sent to hurt good people? By identifying these indicators, that is the life blood of cyber defense; by being able to very quickly recognize them and put them together.

Pulling together this information, it builds on the rules of statistics. We have to understand good behavior and bad behavior to identify anomalies. Identifying those anomalies at the speed of machines will help us in our cyber defense initiatives.

The President's proposal defines the kind of information, specifically, that can be shared and requires very strong protections around privacy and civil liberties to protect our personal information and protect those privacy and civil liberties and American ways of life that we seek to protect and defend through our cybersecurity mission.

The proposal narrowly defines categories of technical information used to define and mitigate these threats so that we can then pull them together. But it does not, for an example, include exfiltrated information; which means the information, for example, that someone might have tried to steal, which could include proprietary information or someone's private information. So very narrowly-defined information on what we need to share and share quickly.

The President's ISAO Executive Order will enhance the information-sharing efforts. The order focuses specifically on encouraging the formation effectiveness of information sharing and analysis organizations. They can be profit or nonprofit, private sector, and they can be composed of any combination of public and private sectors. The Executive Order directs DHS to strongly encourage the development of these formations to bring people together in trusted relationships to share information that transcends competition to enable those cyber threat indicators to come together and show us, again at machine speed, what enemy might be trying to hurt our systems and be able to see at that 50,000-foot level all over the world what actions are happening dispersed that we could use to protect somebody right now.

DHS—this is a very important point—is already sharing information in real time with Federal agencies and the private sector. We share with people and machines using people and machines. We provide information to detect and block cybersecurity threats to our Federal civilian government agencies and, as the under secretary mentioned, within that, using Government-Classified information.

We also provide information to commercial companies so that they can better protect themselves as well, also with some systems using that Classified information. We maintain key trusted information-sharing partnerships at a scientist level and at policy levels with parts of the private sector so we can enable us—ourselves and them to understand what is the science and what are the key things we need to be looking for? So trust between people and machines.

Where are we going and why is this so important? We need to up our game to automate. We need to take the machines and remember that machines are not smart, they are just fast, and use that very machine speed that the adversary uses to steal and hurt us in our cyber systems and use that machine to understand what is happening all over the world and enable our machines in addition to other technologies to sense bad behavior before it hurts.

In doing that, part of that is pulling those automated cyber threat indicators together so that we can start looking at behavior all over the world and work—and this is very, very important—in partnership. So no one can do this alone. We need DHS, we need the FBI, we need the Secret Service, we need the intelligence community, and we need the private sector.

I thank you, Chairman, as well for all the work you have done with the private sector to engage them with your committee and how important it is to work with Government.

We have developed a common language and a common way of writing cyber threat indicators so that anyone who wants to share with us can, that can be transported at machine speed, and that machines can readily read the information; and it limits itself to what is required to be a cyber threat indicator. We need to continue to work with our privacy and civil liberties experts constantly; with the FBI, with the Secret Service, with law enforcement, with the intelligence community to manage all the expectations and all of the equities.

But we are building protocols and structured language to equalize and normalize with what a cyber threat indicator is, to have the machines get a lot of the noise out of the way so our top minds can look at the most egregious threats, and to have our networks become more self-healing and more resilient.

Finally, I would like to reemphasize the importance of our NCCIC, our National Cybersecurity Communications Integration Center, and point out that that is the interface for sharing cyber information across the Government and private sector. But we do this in clear cooperation, and as we develop these protocols, it is with the Secret Service and the FBI and all the law enforcement and the intelligence community and the private sector.

This can't work if we do it alone. It has to respect everyone's equities and all privacy and civil liberties. Having that single designated entity in the Government reduces complexity, as the under secretary stated and streamlines our ability to develop that common picture of the threats we see daily.

Thank you for this opportunity to testify. I look forward to any questions you might have.

Chairman MCCAUL. Thank you. Just let me say that you have really done an outstanding job standing up the NCCIC, bringing the capabilities of the NCCIC to the current threats that we have. Your experience at McAfee is well-served. I thank the Department.

With that, the Chairman now recognizes Dr. Fischer.

STATEMENT OF ERIC A. FISCHER, SENIOR SPECIALIST, SCIENCE AND TECHNOLOGY, CONGRESSIONAL RESEARCH SERVICE, LIBRARY OF CONGRESS

Mr. FISCHER. Good afternoon, Chairman McCaul, Ranking Member Thompson, and distinguished Members of the committee.

On behalf of the Congressional Research Service, I would like to thank you for the opportunity to testify today on information sharing and cybersecurity. Barriers to sharing of cybersecurity information are considered by many, as we heard, to be a significant hindrance to effective protection of information systems.

That is especially true for critical infrastructure, even though most recent prominent cases of successful cyber attacks have not involved such organizations. Many examples have been cited of legal, technical, and other barriers. In addition, traditional approaches to security and confidentiality would themselves impede sharing of information.

There is some disagreement among experts about whether Federal legislation is needed. Nevertheless, there appears to be a fairly broad consensus that legislation could be useful if crafted appropriately. However, there is disagreement also about what the key characteristics should be. Proposals to reduce or remove barriers have raised concerns, some of which are related to the purpose of the barriers; that the barriers are thought to currently impede sharing.

A key challenge appears to be how to achieve the proper level of balance that fosters the sharing of useful information efficiently and effectively, while ensuring avoidance of adverse impacts. I will touch on five questions that the debate has tended to focus on.

Question No. 1: What are the kinds of information for which barriers to sharing make effective cybersecurity more difficult? Information sharing can involve a wide variety of materials communicated on a wide variety of time scales. The level of sensitivity of information can vary. For example, it may be Classified, proprietary, or personal, or open public information. Information of any class will also vary in its value for cybersecurity and the degree to which it needs human processing to be useful.

To the extent that the goal of information sharing is to defend information systems against cyber attacks, the focus has been on actionable information. Such information may often need to be shared very quickly, as Dr. Schneck has mentioned, with little or no time for human examination.

Broader information contributing to shared situational awareness may also be useful; for example, among companies within a sector. Such information might not be technically actionable, but helps organizations to analyze their current security postures and inform their responses.

A key point is that addressing what should be shared, how and when, is not as straightforward as it may seem. This is true not only for cybersecurity information, but more broadly with security information.

Question No. 2: How should information sharing be structured to ensure that it is efficient and effective? Information sharing can conceivably lead to information overload. That can include not only information of uncertain quality and use, but also similar or redundant information from a variety of sources.

Various legislative proposals have approached the structure information sharing differently. The White House proposal would use information sharing and analysis organizations, which were created in the Homeland Security Act, but few of which appear to exist today. It might be useful to clarify the roles of these and other entities as the committee considers legislation.

Question No. 3: What are the risks to privacy rights and civil liberties of individual citizens, and how are they best protected? Such concerns have been a significant source of controversy and debate about information sharing and legislation. They have arisen in part because proposals would permit sharing of specific information or specified information by covered private entities, notwithstanding any other provision of law. That particular phrase has certain implications that would be worthy of—perhaps of additional consideration. Now, the various legislative proposals address privacy concerns in various ways, but there are also many similarities among them.

Fourth question is: What, if any, statutory protections against liability are needed? Concerns about liability has often been cited as a significant barrier to private-sector information sharing, both with other private entities and with the Federal Government. There are—in addition to the notwithstanding provisions, there are also various proposals to prohibit court actions to protect organizations against such actions—or against liability concerns and reduce that barrier.

The fifth question, finally, is: What improvements to current standards and practices are needed to ensure that information sharing is useful and efficient for protecting information systems, networks, and their contents? As the other witnesses have testified, standards for exchange of threat data have been developed and their use is growing. But there are also calls for additional standards and best practices. There are some concerns among observers that such work is needed, particularly with respect to—well, for example, evaluating the effectiveness of information sharing.

That concludes my testimony. Once again, thank you for asking me to appear before you today.

[The prepared statement of Mr. Fischer follows:]

PREPARED STATEMENT OF ERIC A. FISCHER

FEBRUARY 25, 2015

Chairman McCaul, Ranking Member Thompson, and distinguished Members of the committee: Thank you for this opportunity to discuss legislative proposals on information sharing in cybersecurity.[1] In January of this year, the White House announced a revision of its 2011 information-sharing proposal as part of a set of updated proposals and other actions relating to cybersecurity:[2]

- A draft bill to enhance information sharing on cybersecurity within the private sector and between the private sector and the Federal Government. Most of my testimony today will focus on this proposal and related bills in the 113th and 114th Congresses.[3]
- A draft bill to amend Federal statutes relating to cyber crime by creating or increasing criminal penalties for certain types of offenses and providing some other authorities to law-enforcement agencies and the courts.[4]
- A draft bill to harmonize State laws requiring companies holding personal information on customers to notify them of data breaches involving such information.[5]
- A 5-year, $25 million grant to create a new cybersecurity consortium consisting of 13 Historically Black Colleges and Universities (HBCUs), the Lawrence Livermore and Sandia National Laboratories of the Department of Energy, and a South Carolina school district. The object of the program is to help fill de-

[1] This statement is limited to a policy analysis of the proposals and initiatives discussed and is not intended to reach any legal conclusions regarding them.
[2] The White House, "Securing Cyberspace: President Obama Announces New Cybersecurity Legislative Proposal and Other Cybersecurity Efforts," Press Release (January 13, 2015), http://www.whitehouse.gov/the-press-office/2015/01/13/securing-cyberspace-president-obama-announces-new-cybersecurity-legislat.
[3] The White House, Updated Information Sharing Legislative Proposal, 2015, http://www.whitehouse.gov/sites/default/files/omb/legislative/letters/updated-information-sharing-legislative-proposal.pdf.
[4] The White House, Updated Administration Proposal: Law Enforcement Provisions, 2015, http://www.whitehouse.gov/sites/default/files/omb/legislative/letters/updated-law-enforcement-tools.pdf.
[5] The White House, The Personal Data Notification & Protection Act, 2015, http://www.whitehouse.gov/sites/default/files/omb/legislative/letters/updated-data-breach-notification.pdf.

mand for cybersecurity professionals while diversifying the pipeline of talent for this and related fields of expertise.[6] This program can be seen as a complement to legislation enacted by the 113th Congress that addresses cybersecurity workforce needs in the Department of Homeland Security[7] (DHS) and more broadly.[8]

The announcement also included a description of the White House cybersecurity summit held on February 13 at Stanford University.

Barriers to the sharing of information on threats, attacks, vulnerabilities, and other aspects of cybersecurity—both within and across sectors—have long been considered by many to be a significant hindrance to effective protection of information systems, especially those associated with critical infrastructure.[9] Examples have included legal barriers, concerns about liability and misuse, protection of trade secrets and other proprietary business information, and institutional and cultural factors— for example, the traditional approach to security tends to emphasize secrecy and confidentiality, which would necessarily impede sharing of information.

A few sectors are subject to Federal notification requirements,[10] but most such information sharing is voluntary, often through sector-specific Information Sharing and Analysis Centers (ISACs)[11] or programs under the auspices of the Department of Homeland Security (DHS) or sector-specific agencies.[12]

While there is some disagreement among experts about whether Federal legislation is needed to address the problem, there appears to be fairly broad consensus that such legislation could be useful if crafted appropriately but potentially harmful if not. However, there is disagreement about what the key characteristics of useful legislation would be. Proposals to reduce or remove such barriers, including provisions in legislative proposals in the last two Congresses, have raised concerns, some of which are related to the purpose of barriers that currently impede sharing. Examples include risks to individual privacy and even free speech and other rights, use of information for purposes other than cybersecurity, such as unrelated Government regulatory actions, commercial exploitation of personal information, or anticompetitive collusion among businesses that would currently violate Federal law.

More broadly, debate has tended to focus on questions such as the following:

1. What are the kinds of information for which barriers to sharing exist that make effective cybersecurity more difficult, and what are those barriers?

2. How should information sharing be structured in the public and private sectors to ensure that it is efficient and effective?

3. What are the risks to privacy rights and civil liberties of individual citizens associated with sharing different kinds of cybersecurity information, and how can those rights and liberties best be protected?

4. What, if any, statutory protections against liability are needed to reduce disincentives for private-sector entities to share cybersecurity information with

---

[6] The White House, "Vice President Biden Announces $25 Million in Funding for Cybersecurity Education at HBCUs," Press Release (January 15, 2015), *http://www.whitehouse.gov/the-press-office/2015/01/15/vice-president-biden-announces-25-million-funding-cybersecurity-educatio.*

[7] H.R. 2952, the Cybersecurity Workforce Assessment Act (Pub. L. No. 113–246), and S. 1691, the Border Patrol Agent Pay Reform Act of 2014 (Pub. L. No. 113–277), requiring assessments of workforce needs within the Department of Homeland Security and providing enhanced authorities to the Secretary for recruitment and retention of cybersecurity personnel.

[8] S. 1353, the Cybersecurity Enhancement Act of 2014 (Pub. L. No. 113–274), establishing in statute a National Science Foundation program for educating cybersecurity professionals for Government agencies, and an interagency program of challenges and competitions in cybersecurity to stimulate identification and recruitment of cybersecurity professionals more broadly as well as cybersecurity research and innovation.

[9] See, for example, The Markle Foundation Task Force on National Security in the Information Age, *Nation At Risk: Policy Makers Need Better Information to Protect the Country,* March 2009, *http://www.markle.org/downloadable_assets/20090304_mtf_report.pdf;* CSIS Commission on Cybersecurity for the 44th Presidency, *Cybersecurity Two Years Later,* January 2011, *http://csis.org/files/publication/110128_Lewis_CybersecurityTwoYearsLater_Web.pdf.*

[10] Notable examples include the chemical industry, electricity, financial, and transportation sectors.

[11] See, for example, ISAC Council, "National Council of ISACS," 2015, *http://www.isaccouncil.org/.* ISACs were originally formed pursuant to a 1998 Presidential Directive (The White House, "Presidential Decision Directive 63: Critical Infrastructure Protection," May 22, 1998, *http://www.fas.org/irp/offdocs/pdd/pdd-63.htm).*

[12] See also CRS Report R42114, *Federal Laws Relating to Cybersecurity: Overview and Discussion of Proposed Revisions,* by Eric A. Fischer; CRS Report R42409, *Cybersecurity: Selected Legal Issues,* by Edward C. Liu et al.; CRS Report R42984, *The 2013 Cybersecurity Executive Order: Overview and Considerations for Congress,* by Eric A. Fischer et al.; CRS Report R4381, *Legislation to Facilitate Cybersecurity Information Sharing: Economic Analysis,* by N. Eric Weiss.

each other and with Government agencies, and how can the need to reduce such barriers best be balanced against any risks to well-established protections?

5. What improvements to current standards and practices are needed to ensure that information sharing is useful and efficient for protecting information systems, networks, and their contents?

The White House information-sharing proposal would attempt to address such questions in several ways. The discussion below includes a summary of how the proposal would address them in comparison to the following bills addressing information sharing:

- H.R. 234, the Cyber Intelligence Sharing and Protection Act (CISPA), in the 114th Congress, identical to H.R. 624 as passed by the House in the 113th Congress;
- S. 2588, Cybersecurity Information Sharing Act of 2014 (CISA) as reported to the Senate in the 113th Congress;
- S. 456, the Cyber Threat Sharing Act of 2015, as introduced in the 114th Congress.

KINDS OF INFORMATION SHARED

Information sharing can involve a wide variety of material communicated on a wide range of time scales, ranging from broad cybersecurity policies and principles to best practices to descriptions of specific threats and vulnerabilities to computer-generated data transmitted directly from one information system to another electronically. The level of sensitivity of information can also vary—for example, it may be Classified, proprietary, or personal. Information of any class will also vary in its value for cybersecurity and the degree to which it needs human processing to be useful.[13]

To the extent that the goal of information sharing is to defend information systems against cyber attacks, there appears to be a consensus that shared information needs to be actionable—that is, it should identify or evoke a specific response aimed at mitigating cybersecurity risks. To be meaningfully actionable, information may often need to be shared very quickly or even in an automated fashion. There may therefore be little or no time for human operators to examine a specific parcel of data to determine whether sharing it could raise privacy, liability, or other concerns.

The White House proposal would limit the scope of shared information covered under the proposal to "cyber threat indicators," which includes information needed to "indicate, describe, or identify" malicious reconnaissance or command-and-control activities, methods of social engineering and of defeating technical or operational controls, and technical vulnerabilities, and from which "reasonable efforts" have been made to remove personally identifying information if the person is thought to be unrelated to the threat. The definition in S. 456 is largely identical.

The definition in the White House proposal and S. 456 are arguably the narrowest in scope. S. 2588 also focuses on "cyber threat indicators," with a definition that is similar to that in the White House proposal, but is somewhat broader, including other attributes, such as the actual or potential harm caused by an incident. It also expressly permits sharing of information on countermeasures—measures to prevent or mitigate threats and vulnerabilities.

H.R. 234 uses the term "cyber threat information," characterized as information "directly pertaining to" efforts to gain unauthorized access to information systems or to effect negative impacts on systems or networks, threats to the information security of a system or its contents, and vulnerabilities of systems and networks. The bill also defines a related term, "cyber threat intelligence," with characteristics similar to those of cyber threat information but is in the possession of the intelligence community.

STRUCTURE OF INFORMATION SHARING

Information sharing can conceivably lead to information overload, where an entity receives much more information than it can reasonably process. That could include not only information of uncertain quality and use, but also similar or redundant information from a variety of sources. In addition, a proliferation of sharing mechanisms could lead to stovepiping, which could reduce sharing across sectors, for example, and lack of clarity with respect to responsibilities, which could lead to gaps in sharing useful information. In contrast, a narrow, tightly-defined structure for in-

---

[13] See, for example, Kathleen M. Moriarty, "Transforming Expectations for Threat-Intelligence Sharing," RSA Perspective (August 3, 2013), *https://www.emc.com/collateral/emc-perspective/h12175-transf-expect-for-threat-intell-sharing.pdf*.

formation sharing could lead to logjams or impede innovation in response to continuing evolution of cyberspace.

The White House proposal and S. 456 would create a structure for information sharing that includes the National Cybersecurity and Communications Integration Center (NCCIC) as the Federal hub for receipt and distribution of cybersecurity information, and fostering the use of private information sharing and analysis organizations (ISAOs) as recipients of information from private entities.[14] ISAOs could presumably also share such information under the provisions of the Homeland Security Act, but the proposal does not specifically address that function for them. The proposal would require the DHS Secretary to ensure that indicators are shared in a timely fashion with other Federal agencies. S. 456 would require that procedures for such sharing be established and would specifically require the Secretary to ensure that both useful Classified and Unclassified information is shared with non-Federal entities.

H.R. 234 would create an entity at DHS (presumably the NCCIC[15]) to share threat information and an entity at the Department of Justice to share cyber crime information. It would require individual agencies that receive threat information to develop procedures for sharing it. In contrast to S. 456, it would require the Director of National Intelligence to establish procedures for sharing Classified threat information. It would also designate specific classes of private-sector entities as those permitted to monitor systems and share threat information under the bill. Those include entities that provide cybersecurity goods and services to others or to themselves.

S. 2588 would require DHS to create a "capability and process" for sharing both threat indicators and countermeasures. It would establish an interagency process to develop procedures for sharing Federal information with the private sector. It would require development of an interagency process for sharing Classified threat indicators.

TIMELINESS OF SHARING

The time scale on which shared information will be most useful varies. That is especially an issue in an environment where the relevance of timing for shared information may be measured in seconds or even milliseconds in many cases.[16] The White House proposal and S. 456 would address this concern by requiring the NCCIC to share indicators "in as close to real time as practicable" and by requiring establishment of a program to advance automated mechanisms for such sharing.

H.R. 234 and S. 2588 would also require "real-time sharing." The meaning of this term is not explicitly defined or described in the bills, but it presumably refers to sharing that occurs rapidly, for example, by machine-to-machine transmission. That is consistent with the stated purposes of the legislative proposals, in that threat information would likely need to be disseminated quickly in order to detect or prevent incoming cyber attacks, which can occur very quickly. This raises the question of whether this term should require any particular mode of sharing, for example, by machine-to-machine transmission without or with minimal intervening processing by human operators, and how different interpretations of the term may impact operational effectiveness, privacy interests, and competition for technical and financial resources. The White House proposal appears to address that through its proposed development of automated mechanisms, and S. 2588 would require development of a process to receive indicators and countermeasures electronically, including via an "automated process between information systems."

---

[14] ISAOs were defined in the Homeland Security Act (6 U.S.C. § 131(5)) as entities that gather and analyze information relating to the security of critical infrastructure, communicate such information to help with defense against and recovery from incidents, and disseminate such information to any entities that might assist in carrying out those goals. The proposal covers receipt of indicators by ISAOs but does not mention communication or dissemination of information by them, except, by inference, to the NCCIC. Information Sharing and Analysis Centers (ISACs) are more familiar to most observers. They may also be ISAOs but are not the same, having been originally formed pursuant to a 1998 Presidential directive (The White House, "Presidential Decision Directive 63: Critical Infrastructure Protection," May 22, 1998, *http://www.fas.org/irp/offdocs/pdd/pdd-63.htm*).

[15] The text in the bill was originally drafted before the enactment of the National Cybersecurity and Communications Integration Center Act of 2014 (Pub. L. No. 113–282), which established the NCCIC by statute.

[16] See, for example, M.J. Herring and K.D. Willett, "Active Cyber Defense: A Vision for Real-Time Cyber Defense," *Journal of Information Warfare* 13, no. 2 (April 2014): 46–55.

PRIVACY AND CIVIL LIBERTIES

Concerns relating to privacy and civil liberties, especially the protection of personal and proprietary information and uses of shared information, have been a significant source of controversy in debate about information-sharing legislation. Such concerns have arisen in part because the White House proposal and the bills would permit sharing of specified cybersecurity information by covered private entities "notwithstanding any other provision of law." That would arguably remove barriers to sharing stemming from concerns that information would inadvertently violate laws such as those on privacy and anti-trust.

However, it also raises concerns about privacy and civil liberties. In particular, personally identifying information might be included in the shared information but might not be related to the threat. In addition, data analytics might conceivably be used to draw inferences about identity from data sets even if any given piece of the shared information would not be identifying. Second, if access to shared information is not strictly controlled and restricted, or is used for purposes other than cybersecurity, risks to civil liberties may arise. Concerns have also been raised about regulatory use of shared information and disclosure of proprietary business information.

The White House proposal would address such concerns by:
- limiting application of the "notwithstanding" provision to indicators disclosed to the NCCIC and ISAOs;
- limiting private-sector use of shared indicators to purposes relating to protection of information systems and their contents;
- requiring minimization of personally identifiable information and safeguarding of any such information that cannot be removed;
- requiring development of guidelines by the Attorney General on limiting the acquisition and sharing of personally identifiable information and establishing processes for anonymization, safeguarding, and destruction of information;
- exempting information received by the Federal Government from disclosure under the Freedom of Information Act;
- prohibiting use of shared information for regulatory enforcement;
- requiring penalties for Federal violations of its restrictions relating to information sharing; and
- an annual report to Congress on privacy and civil liberties.

S. 456 includes those provisions but would also permit a private entity to receive indicators under the "notwithstanding" provision.

H.R. 234 and S. 2588 have related provisions except as follows: Both bills explicitly limit Federal use of shared information to cybersecurity purposes and uses relating to protection of individuals and investigation and prosecution of cyber crimes and certain other offenses. They both require various activities to reduce the degree to which personal information is shared and other means of safeguarding it from unauthorized sharing and use. H.R. 234 requires that guidelines be developed through an interagency process.

LIABILITY PROTECTIONS

Concern about liability has often been cited as a significant barrier to private-sector sharing of cybersecurity information, both with other private entities and with the Federal Government. In addition to the protections granted by the use of "notwithstanding any other provision of law" with respect to provision of information by private-sector entities, the White House proposal would address this issue by prohibiting civil or criminal actions in Federal or State courts for covered activities with respect to lawfully obtained cyber threat indicators disclosed to or received from the NCCIC or a certified ISAO. However, it also specifies monopolistic actions such as price fixing that are not permitted.

The prohibition on civil or criminal actions in H.R. 234 covers acquisition and sharing of cyber threat information, or decisions for cybersecurity purposes based on such information. The bill stipulates that actions must be taken in good faith. The S. 2588 prohibition covers only private defendants, and includes monitoring systems or sharing information. S. 2588 states that a good-faith reliance that an activity was permitted under the bill's provisions will serve as a complete defense against any court action. It also stipulates that private-sector exchange of cyber threat information or assistance for cybersecurity purposes does not violate anti-trust laws, but further specifies monopolistic actions such as price-fixing that are not permitted.

IMPROVEMENTS TO STANDARDS AND PRACTICES

The concerns discussed above about what information would be most useful to share and how raise the question of whether better standards and best practices are needed for improving the effectiveness and efficiency of information sharing.[17] The White House proposal and S. 456 would require the DHS Secretary to establish a process for selecting a private entity that would determine best practices for creating and operating private ISAOs. The recent Executive Order on information sharing has a similar provision.[18] There are no similar provisions in the other bills.

Chairman McCAUL. Thank you, Dr. Fischer.

I now recognize myself for questions.

Ms. Spaulding, I think as you mentioned, we have extraordinary offensive capabilities that we—you and I have seen and Dr. Schneck. That kind of capability turned against us could be very destructive. It is the defensive capability that I think is where we are trying to improve here through additional legislation.

I am very proud of this committee's work last Congress in passing really the first cybersecurity legislation, landmark cybersecurity legislation, that I think the Ranking Member—I can speak for him as well—is both pro-security but pro-privacy. We had that support from two groups that don't always agree on how to get things done.

Mr. THOMPSON. Oh, really?

Chairman McCAUL. Well, I am not talking about you. I am talking about the pro-privacy and pro-security.

You know, as I have studied this—and I have studied it extensively—it seems to me that there is—the Department of Homeland Security is really the ideal place for the safe harbor. It is the civilian interface to the private sector. It also has a robust privacy office and can protect personal information.

Some would argue it should be another portal in the Federal Government. I think that the safe harbor at DHS is—again, should be the lead portal, if you will, for the sharing of this information.

But there are other opinions on that. I wanted to elicit first from Dr. Schneck and Ms. Spaulding, what are your thoughts on how to integrate the other portals that exist today? We have, of course, NSA, the intelligence community, we have Treasury Department that the financial world, as I talk to people in that sector seem to—they like that portal, as well. I know that you would be taking it—you know, information from the intelligence community, FBI, and other agencies to basically funnel that threat information through the DHS civilian interface.

But can you speak to these other portals and how they factor into the President's proposal and what do you think would be the best idea here?

Ms. SPAULDING. Yes, thank you, Mr. Chairman.

First, I think it is really important to emphasize what this legislation does and does not cover. So this is narrowly focused on network defense and the kind of information that is most important for specifically defending networks; and that is this cyber threat indicator information. It is in no way intended to get in the way of existing relationships that companies might have today with other

---

[17] See, for example, Moriarty, *Transforming Expectations for Threat-Intelligence Sharing.*
[18] Executive Order 13691, "Promoting Private Sector Cybersecurity Information Sharing," *Federal Register* 80, no. 34 (February 20, 2015): 9349–53.

23

parts of the Federal Government, whether it is the FBI or Treasury or elsewhere in the Federal Government.

Calls to say we think we see something odd going on in our system should continue to be made wherever those companies are most comfortable going in. We have mechanisms in place to ensure that a call to one is effectively and appropriately a call to all; and that we put together the appropriate interagency teams to respond to those kinds of requests for assistance and information coming in.

So this is by no means intended to cover all kinds of information sharing between the private sector and the Government. Those relationships are very important.

Chairman McCAUL. I think that is an important point. As I talk to the private sector—and it is very important to me to have their buy-in on this—I think that is a very important point to make; is that we are not saying you can't have contact with these other portals. It is just that DHS is, you know, the lead interface.

Dr. Schneck, do you have any thoughts on that?

Ms. SCHNECK. I would only add at a technical level, we are working day in and day out with our——

Ms. SPAULDING. Push to talk.

Ms. SCHNECK. Sorry. At a technical level, we are working constantly with our peers, across with the FBI and with the Secret Service and with the intelligence community to look at how do we make sure that information that comes in is handled and distributed exactly the right way in real time, as if it had come into them, so that we can have it. The important thing here is that it is not a fragmented weather map, if you would. The way to see a tornado—and I used to work tornado modeling. The way you do this is to see all the information at once.

That is one of the key reasons why we think this is so important, to have the NCCIC do this. But we are working constantly with our partners to make sure that no one is deprived of any information. That is what takes so long. It is not just a technology problem. This is a policy puzzle of how do we preserve the privacy, civil liberties, and equities, continue to maintain all the existing relationships and make sure information gets to the right people at the right time at light speed.

Chairman McCAUL. Let me just echo the comments made earlier, and that is that in the last 5 years, I have seen the capabilities at Homeland Security go way up. The sharing of this threat information in real time has increased exponentially, I think, under your leadership. That makes a difference. Because there were doubters, you know, 5 years ago about whether DHS could stand up and have that capability. I think you have demonstrated and proved that they can.

So last question. Well, I have two quick ones. But on the liability protection, I commend the Secretary for coming forward with this piece. It is sometimes a bone of contention between both sides of the aisle. But I think it is absolutely essential to incentivize the private sector to participate in the safe harbor; for without that, they will not do so. I think they have to have the assurance that if they share information, they are not open to a lawsuit.

So I have talked to the private sector. They like the liability protections that are presented here. I think they have some concern

24

about private-to-private sharing and the certification process and all this. How would that work under this proposal?

Ms. SPAULDING. So the liability protections, as you know, apply not only to sharing of these cyber threat indicators with the NCCIC, with the Department of Homeland Security, but also to sharing with these information sharing and analysis organizations, these—we call them ISAOs. Many of those are the ISACs that exist today for the various sectors; the financial services ISAC, the multi-State ISAC, and others.

So what the legislation provides is that the private sector can share among themselves through these appropriate organizations and enjoy the same liability protection for providing that information to those organizations.

Chairman MCCAUL. I think the safe harbor at DHS is a construct within—where we want to incentivize most of the sharing of information. But I do think the private sector's private-to-private sharing also should be protected as well. We can discuss that more as this legislation unfolds.

Last question. I get asked this question probably the most. That is, you know, what keeps you up at night? I talk about cybersecurity quite a bit. But within this space, to both Ms. Spaulding and Dr. Schneck, what keeps you up at night the most?

Ms. SPAULDING. So clearly, what I worry most about is cyber activity that would significantly disrupt our critical infrastructure. So we spend a lot of time thinking about those consequences and making sure we understand interdependencies within the physical world. Because this is not just about protecting machines, this is about protecting our ways of life.

So we need to make sure that we understand what are those consequences that would be most devastating, and that we are working most closely with those parts of our critical infrastructure to make sure that we can mitigate those consequences and try to prevent, as Dr. Schneck said, bad things—bad things from doing bad harm.

Chairman MCCAUL. Thank you.

Dr. Schneck.

Ms. SCHNECK. Thank you. I would echo the interface of the physical world. No one ever tried to keep a machine safe to keep a machine safe. Our job at Homeland Security is to keep people safe. The Secretary always tells us that cybersecurity is a key part of homeland security.

Another piece that really does keep me up at night as well is our small-to-medium business and our State and local. They don't typically have enough budget to focus on cybersecurity. Part of the elegance that will come from our teamwork with our partners and the FBI and the intelligence community and across the private sector and Government is to pull those threat indicators together to be able to, in final phases, make them available to the greater 99 percent of our business fabric that is not a big company and to our State and locals, and to have that system learn by participating and make all of us smarter and safer.

If I would just add, I thank you for your gracious comments about my leadership earlier. I think about the team back at the NCCIC and back across DHS that really makes it happen, and I want you to know about that. I walked into the finest team on the planet.

Chairman MCCAUL. Well, thank you. Your boss just arrived. I want to recognize the Secretary. I will reiterate my comments about Ms. Spaulding and Dr. Schneck and their tremendous performance in standing up DHS with the capabilities with the respect it deserves, and I think the ability to move forward with the proposal from you, sir.

I also commended you before you came in on your proposal of liability protection, which I think will incentivize the private sector to fully participate in this safe harbor. So thank you for your leadership. You got two really good employees right here.

So with that, the Chairman now recognizes the Ranking Member.

Mr. THOMPSON. Thank you, Mr. Chairman.

Very rarely do we agree 100 percent on anything. But the two employees referenced here today absolutely have distinguished themselves. Not just here, but in their careers in general.

I would like unanimous consent to have entered into the record the letter that you co-authored with me and our colleagues on the Senate to the President referencing some concerns we had about the new cyber center.

Chairman MCCAUL. Without objection, it is ordered.

[The information follows:]

LETTER SUBMITTED FOR THE RECORD BY RANKING MEMBER BENNIE G. THOMPSON

FEBRUARY 11, 2015.

The Honorable BARACK OBAMA,
President of The United States, The White House, Washington, DC 20500.

DEAR MR. PRESIDENT: Thank you for your dedication and leadership on the important national and economic security issue of cybersecurity. As the leaders of the Committees that developed legislation to codify the Department of Homeland Security's role as the lead Federal agency for helping to protect private sector networks, principally through the National Cybersecurity and Communications Integration Center (NCCIC), we have several questions regarding your newly-unveiled proposal for a new cybersecurity information integration center.

We were pleased that you signed "National Cybersecurity Protection Act of 2014" (P.L. 113–282) into law less than two months ago, on December 18th, and implementation of that law is underway. At this time, the NCCIC, with its newly codified authority, is working to establish itself as an effective partner with the private sector to meet evolving cybersecurity challenges. Pursuant to the "National Cybersecurity Protection Act of 2014," among the functions of the NCCIC are the following:

"(1) being a Federal civilian interface for the multi-directional and cross-sector sharing of information related to cybersecurity risks, incidents, analysis, and warnings for Federal and non-Federal entities;

"(2) providing shared situational awareness to enable real-time, integrated, and operational actions across the Federal Government and non-Federal entities to address cybersecurity risks and incidents to Federal and non-Federal entities;

"(3) coordinating the sharing of information related to cybersecurity risks and incidents across the Federal Government;"

Additionally, the NCCIC is "a 24/7 cyber situational awareness, incident response, and management center that is a national nexus of cyber and communications integration for the Federal government, intelligence community, and law enforcement." We understand that increasing private sector participation and improving the quantity and quality of information received at this Federal civilian center was a priority for you, as it is for us and DHS Secretary Jeh Johnson.

Therefore, we have questions about your new proposal to establish another information sharing hub, the Cyber Threat Intelligence Integration Center (CTIIC) that was unveiled this week, as the activities outlined for the center seem to resemble the functions authorized in law for the NCCIC. We are concerned that the introduction of the CTIIC at this moment in the NCCIC's evolution may complicate those efforts and introduce uncertainty for the private sector and other partners. It also risks driving away activity to the new CTIIC, which would be operated by the Office of the Director of National Intelligence (ODNI).

Accordingly, we request that you please answer the following questions:

- Why is the CTIIC needed at this time? How is it supposed to differ from the NCCIC? Do you intend to submit a legislative proposal to Congress to authorize this center? If so, when?
- Some have observed that functions of the CTIIC are duplicative with those of the NCCIC.[1] Others have said that it introduces unnecessary bureaucracy.[2] Is the CTIIC duplicative? Specifically, what are the responsibilities and activities of the CTIIC and are they already covered by the NCCIC or, for that matter, the FBI's cyber center?
- Why are you establishing this center at the ODNI, particularly in light of your longstanding interest in bolstering DHS as the interface for the private sector on cybersecurity? What interactions will the new center have with the private sector?
- Given that the CTIIC will be housed in the Intelligence Community, please explain how it will relate to the National Security Agency and the degree to which it will be involved in the collection of intelligence?
- As you roll out this new center, how do you plan to ensure that the private sector shares timely cyber threat information with the statutorily-authorized NCCIC?
- To what degree does the effectiveness of the CTIIC depend on enactment of information-sharing legislation? The protections for personally identifiable information are well-established with respect to private sector information sharing at the NCCIC. What, if any, privacy protections would be required for information sharing with the CTIIC?

As partners in efforts to bolster the nation's cyber posture, we have a keen interest in ensuring efficiency and effectiveness of the Federal government's efforts and seek opportunities to minimize duplication and get the best results for our money.

Thank you, in advance, for your timely response to our questions. Should you or other members of your team need to follow up on this request, please feel free to contact Hope Goins, Chief Counsel for Oversight (Committee on Homeland Security, Minority), Brett DeWitt, Senior Policy Advisor for Cybersecurity (Committee on Homeland Security, Majority), Matt Grote, Senior Professional Staff Member (Senate Homeland Security and Governmental Affairs Committee, Minority) or William McKenna, Chief Counsel for Homeland Security (Senate Homeland Security and Governmental Affairs Committee, Majority).

Sincerely,

BENNIE G. THOMPSON,
Ranking Member, Committee on Homeland Security.
MICHAEL T. MCCAUL,
Chairman, Committee on Homeland Security.
THOMAS R. CARPER,
Ranking Member, Homeland Security and Government Affairs Committee.
RON JOHNSON,
Chairman, Homeland Security and Government Affairs Committee.

Mr. THOMPSON. Thank you.

Ms. Spaulding, I referenced the letter in my opening statements. I would hope that at some point we will have an answer back on that. Thank you very much.

---

[1] Sean Lyngaas, "New Cyber Agency Modeled on Counterterrorism Center," FEDERAL COMPUTER WEEK (FCW), February 10, 2015, wrote that Chris Cummiskey, the former DHS under secretary for management, said his first reaction to the news of the CTIIC's establishment was that "its prescribed functions sounded quite a bit like NCCIC's."

[2] Melissa Hathaway, former White House cybersecurity coordinator and president of Hathaway Global Strategies told Ellen Nakashima in "New Agency to Sniff Out Threats in Cyberspace," WASHINGTON POST, February 10, 2015, that said "We should not be creating more organizations and bureaucracy . . . we need to be forcing the existing organizations to become more effective—hold them accountable." Further, Stephen Cobb, a security researcher at ESET North America, told National Public Radio's Marketplace Tech that "the only real difference between NCCIC and CTIIC is that NCCIC reports to the Department of Homeland Security, whereas the new agency answers to the Office of Director of National Intelligence," at *http://www.marketplace.org/topics/tech/two-cybersecurity-agencies-diverged-wood.*

27

In 3 days, unless a miracle happens, we will be, as a Department, out of money. We have talked here about the cyber threat and what that means to this country, what keeps us up at night and all of that.

Ms. Spaulding, can you enlighten the Members of this committee, if 3 days come and DHS is without money to go forward, what that would mean for our cyber defense here?

Ms. SPAULDING. Absolutely, Ranking Member Thompson. Thank you, and let me just reassure you that we are working diligently on the response to your letter, and it will arrive promptly. It is a priority of the Secretary's that we be prompt in our response to Congressional inquires. This is one we take particularly seriously. We will get back to you very quickly on that.

With regard to the impact of a potential funding hiatus, I can say it will—as I said in my testimony, it will have an impact on our cyber mission. Let me give you a few examples. So we are in the process of deploying the latest iteration of our sensors in the dot.gov, in our civilian government networks and systems. That is our Einstein program. This is Einstein 3A, which is the technology that will help us not just detect, but block the intrusions coming in; and Einstein 2, which is the detection capability.

These activities of rolling this out will have to stop in the event of a funding hiatus. I will say a week of stoppage we could probably make up. But with each week that continues, that is another couple of agencies that are not brought on-board and receiving the protection at a time when the adversary is not taking any break in their efforts to penetrate our civilian government systems.

Our other dot.gov technologies is our continuous diagnostics and mitigation program, which looks inside that civilian government networks and systems to look at their health. That—deployment of that also will be delayed if we have a funding hiatus. That has an impact on our ability to quickly address—identify and address vulnerabilities like the JASBUG vulnerability that has been most recently in the media.

With regard to our enhanced cybersecurity services program, where we make sensitive Government and Classified information available to cybersecurity providers to better protect private-sector companies, the on-boarding of new providers will be delayed if we have a funding hiatus. So our ability to protect critical infrastructure owners and operators will be impacted.

On the communications side, our ability to keep up with the next generation of communication technologies that the private sector is going full-speed-ahead to implement, our ability to continue to provide priority interoperable communication for National security and emergency response will be impacted, will be delayed. As I say, in the mean time, the private sector is rolling out that new technology. If we don't keep up, we will not be able to provide that prioritized interoperable communications that is so essential.

Mr. THOMPSON. Well, thank you very much. A follow-up to that, all of us want to work with the business community. What constraints would a lack of money impact the Department's work in interfacing from a cyber standpoint with the business community?

Ms. SPAULDING. So the work we do on a daily basis to build those essential trusted relationships would be put on hold. All of that outreach, we are—have done a campaign across the country, for example, to educate critical infrastructure owners and operators about threats to their industrial control systems in cyber space. Critically important; you asked what keeps me awake at night, those are the kinds of things that do. Those activities would not be able to continue.

The guidance from the President, the direction to the President to have—for the Department to set up the standards body to facilitate the establishment of these appropriate information-sharing mechanisms between private-sector entities, these information sharing and analysis organizations, our ability to issue that grant and get that going forward would be hampered by both a continuing resolution and certainly by a funding hiatus.

Mr. THOMPSON. Thank you, Mr. Chairman. I yield back.

Chairman MCCAUL. Let me just say for myself that I don't think we should be playing politics with the National Security Agency, given the high-threat environment that we are in today, both from a cybersecurity standpoint and also from al-Qaeda and ISIS, as well. I certainly hope that Congress can resolve this and avoid a shutdown of the Department.

With that, the Chairman now recognizes Mr. Clawson.

Mr. CLAWSON. Thank you for coming today and for your service. Thank you—both of y'all for holding this important session.

So I imagine myself on the top of a large multi-national company. I have got employee—I have got stakeholders all over the world, a board of directors that is not all Americans. I have got an ERP system, maybe it is—could be Triton Bond, could be Oracle, could be—you know, could be SAP, could be anything. I have worked years to get it integrated around the world. Factories everywhere. I accept that cybersecurity is an important public good, and that if we don't have it, we are dead. I also accept that the liability insurance that you y'all talk about here protects one stakeholder, and that is the shareholder.

But my world is much more complicated. I have data centers, regional data centers, all over the world, with customers and suppliers integrated in those data centers. Now as CEO, I am gonna go out and say look, y'all, in the name of cybersecurity for the world, but mainly for America, we are gonna start sharing data. You kind of have to trust us on what we are gonna share, when we are gonna share it. The devil will be in the details actually. We are gonna—you know, those specifics will be defined later. But don't worry, none of this data will get into the wrong hands; your privacy will not be violated, even though you grew up in the Czech Republic or Russia, where they were spied upon their whole lives, and the last thing they want is another big brother.

It feels to me like y'all got a tough sale. It feels to me liability insurance or not, that my world is all about multiple stakeholders. It is not just about profit; big, bad corporations making more money. We are trying to protect our customers, our suppliers, the communities that we live in. What I have read so far about what y'all propose just doesn't feel like a very compelling case that I can take to my multi-national board of directors.

What am I missing, and what data can you give to make this more palatable? Because if you can't get me, I know what my friends back in the private sector are gonna say. It is not just about profit. Go ahead.

Ms. SPAULDING. No, Congressman, you have very well articulated the concerns that we hear when we are out talking to our partners in the private sector. You are absolutely right. There is a wide range of reasons that companies have—legitimate reasons—for having concerns about sharing information with the Government.

Mr. CLAWSON. It is not just lack—it is not lack of patriotism.

Ms. SPAULDING. Right. No, I totally agree. Throughout my career, interacting with CEOs of companies, I find them to be an extremely patriotic bunch. So I absolutely agree.

I will say, with respect to this legislative proposal and the sharing of cyber threat indicator information, you are correct, the devil is in the details. The good news is that as we move to automated information sharing, those details will be apparent. There will be total transparency about the specific kinds of information that we are seeking and receiving.

Because we are creating a structured way of presenting that information that will detail very specifically the kind of information that we want to get. We will also work through the policy and protocols for protecting that sensitive information, both in terms of proprietary information and privacy information. So those things will be transparent.

Mr. CLAWSON. Can you imagine if, in one of the countries that I operate in, the government of that country telling me that I had to share this same sort of information? How would we respond?

Ms. SPAULDING. Again, I—think the—limiting this to cyber threat indicator information, which is fairly technical information about the IP addresses that are sending malware, for example, to disrupt equipment, this is the kind of information that is less sensitive. Each company will make its own decisions. I think you are right.

One of the things we have tried to be clear about, this is not a silver bullet, this is not a panacea, this is not gonna make every company open its doors. But it does address concerns that we have heard from the private sector. There will be a fair amount of detail about precisely what we are talking about sharing here. The legislation defines it fairly——

Mr. CLAWSON. I think that without that detail, any private-sector CEO would be negligent to go along on the basis of trust.

Chairman MCCAUL. Dr. Schneck, would you like to answer that?

Ms. SCHNECK. Yes, very briefly. So I was in a very large company about 18 months ago. I hear you. I lived that. I was not at the level you describe. But I was a key technology officer for the global government. I was the one that shared information or didn't. I was the subject of a storied phone call from a former FBI executive and executive assistant director, three down from the top, who I consider a very close friend, who yelled at me at 11:00 at night on my home phone because he found out something he didn't know, and I couldn't share it with him.

We are going to have to earn your trust. This sharing is not required. It is my scientific belief that there will be benefits in getting our data. You don't have to give anything at first to get it. I think what the under secretary points out is very important, it is

key. These are just scientific indicators. But you—the companies
will see that. We will work to earn your trust. It is voluntary.

Mr. CLAWSON. I am nonpartisan on this issue. Anything I can do
to help you, you know, with my background, I urge you to seek me
out. I am always worried about people on the telephone. I am even
more worried about people in my ERP system. So with that as a
starting point, y'all—you know, use—anything I can do to help, I
am here.

Ms. SPAULDING. Thank you very much, Congressman. We will
definitely take you up on that. Thank you.

Chairman McCAUL. If the gentleman would yield, we do have a
field trip, if you will, to the NCCIC facility. I would encourage you
to attend that. I think it is important to note also this is not a
mandatory sharing system. It is voluntary. This authorization that
we authorized the Department's cyber operations last Congress had
the support of industry, the chamber, the privacy groups.

All I think in moving forward what we want to do is provide liability protection so that they can fully participate. Because I think
there is a reluctance, as you point out. Because you have a duty
to the shareholders to not want to participate until you have that
assurance that you wouldn't open yourself up to a lawsuit. So I
look forward to you—you obviously have tremendous experience on
this issue. I look forward to working with you on this.

Chairman recognizes the gentlelady from Texas, Ms. Jackson
Lee.

Ms. JACKSON LEE. Mr. Chairman, thank you very much. I might
say to my good friend, Mr. Clawson, with his experience but also
his demeanor. I truly believe that we have common ground on
these very important issues.

I gave an old story that I hope will be very brief. I indicated that
when I chaired the transportation security committee, we had included infrastructure, which was then cybersecurity. The point was
that it was all embracing an infrastructure that we had not yet hit,
if you will, the epicenter of fear and epicenter of hacking. But we
did look at the infrastructures that are governed by cybersecurity
and realized that we were vulnerable.

So I want to thank all of you for bringing us up into the 21st
Century as it relates to home homeland security and this very cru-
cial issue. I want to add my appreciation for those of you who have
come from the private sector for serving your Nation.

Let me acknowledge the Secretary in his absence and thank him
for being, as he has indicated, everywhere and all over on the basis
of National security.

I want to thank the Chairman of this full committee. I hope that
his efforts will be heard in his Republican conference that we
should be dealing with National security and not political security.
Clearly, on the issue of where we are in this time and date and
what we are facing, I can't imagine a more important component.
There are many important components at DHS. But certainly,
what we are discussing today has far-reaching impact.

So I want to just take the words that were presented when the
President offered his thoughts on January 13 and he said when
public and private networks are facing an unprecedented threat
from rogue hackers, as well as organized crime and even state ac-

tors, the President is, of course, unveiling the next steps in his plan to defend the Nation.

At that time, then he unveiled the White House proposal. That is, of course, the Cyber Threat Intelligence Integration Center. Many of you know that we have worked so hard on the efforts to have the National Cybersecurity and Communications Integration Center.

So my questions are going to be—I know we had some earlier discussions—the pointed synergism, if you will, of those two entities and the concern about confusion between the broader public. My interpretation—I have some privacy questions—is that the CTIIC will be not gathering, but analyzing; will be the high-level threat entity. My concern is, will that information of their analysis be accessible to DHS, Members of the respective homeland security committees? Because it looks as if there is an attempt to put a wall between the very agency that then has to act on trying to save the Nation.

Then, of course, the NCCIC will be the face to the private sector. We will have to engender their trust. They will have to know well, this is an agency that can help me, or do I need to try to bang down the doors of the CTIIC, even though that is not the intent?

So let me just end right there so that I can ask you, Madam Secretary Spaulding, our Ranking Member gave you the opportunity for a long litany. Let me for the record speak to this defunding or no funding of Department of Homeland Security in the backdrop of—let me try not to use the word "crisis"—but the increasing threats that are viable through hacking, through other efforts as it relates to security.

Does this put us, the Department of Homeland Security and the security of this Nation, in a position of jeopardy if all of the functions in your area are either halted, stalled, people laid off because of the actual moment in history that we are in? Are we at a serious moment in history that you need all hands on deck?

Ms. SPAULDING. Congresswoman, I think that is an accurate statement. I mean, we are—as this committee knows as well as anyone, we are, as I said, under daily moment-by-moment efforts by adversaries to penetrate our networks and systems across the Federal Government, State, local, territorial, Tribal government systems, and the private sector.

There is no pausing, no slowing down, in that range of actors' efforts to penetrate our systems and to do us harm. So anything that hampers, we are running on a daily basis full speed ahead to try to keep ahead of those—efforts of those adversaries. Anything that hampers and slows us down creates risk for us and for the Nation.

Ms. JACKSON LEE. If I could get these last two questions in, I would greatly appreciate it.

I started out by offering my assessment of the CTIC—CTIIC and the NCCIC. So if I could get the question answered as to how the public is to decipher between these entities. Then I want to add a question of my colleague here on privacy.

Will the information shared that is going to be shared with the Government identify the identity of law-abiding citizens? Will it be the responsibility of the company—companies—for removing personal information for what is shared with DHS?

So first, how are they gonna interface with these two entities? I am concerned about the confusion. Then the privacy question.

Ms. SPAULDING. Great. I very much appreciate the question. We welcome the establishment of the Cyber Threat Intelligence Integration Center. Those two "I"s are actually important to help make this distinction. Because what the CTIIC will do for us is to pull together intelligence information from across the 16 different entities that make up that intelligence community over which the DNI, the Director of National Intelligence, has purview.

So that is a very useful function for us. Part of their articulated, explicit mission is to support the NCCIC, our operations in watch center, and the other centers across Government; the FBI's NCIJTF and the other centers out there across Government. They are—in military terms, they are supporting command and we are the supported demand. So they will provide that integrated analysis for us, which will be very useful.

They also will be one place where we can go to work with the intelligence community to get information cleared for wide dissemination. So whether that is continuing to press intelligence agencies to write or release, to create products from the very beginning that can be widely disseminated or to go back to them to get things declassified that we think are important to disseminate widely. Instead of having to go to 16 different entities, we can go to this one place who will be an advocate for us, because that is their mission in making sure we can disseminate this information.

Those two key functions will be really helpful for us. It is a very distinct mission from our mission, which is to interact with the private sector. That is not the mission of the CTIIC. Our mission is to interact on a daily basis with our partners across the Federal Government and the private sector and to receive information from them; and most importantly, to get information out as broadly as we the can so that those who are trying to defend their networks can do so effectively.

I will ask the deputy to address the privacy issue if——

Mr. CLAWSON [presiding]. Quickly, if that is okay.

Ms. SCHNECK. I will make it very quick, sir.

The privacy issue cuts to the core of why we do what we do and why I came here to the Department to serve in Government. The story I shared about the call from the FBI, this is one of the finest investigators on the planet. I wanted to answer him. I couldn't. If we had a system like this in place that night, I could have. My lawyer would have given us the ability to share just the indicators. So what we are building——

Mr. CLAWSON. That I understand.

Ms. SCHNECK. So what we are building is with a team, working every day with the FBI, their assistant director of cyber. He called me last night just to make sure we were in the loop on things. This is the kind of relationship that we have. He called me on my cell phone a couple of weeks ago. We have——

Ms. JACKSON LEE. Are you answering—I am sorry. I don't want to interrupt. But are you answering my question, which is will the information——

Ms. SCHNECK. Yes.

Ms. JACKSON LEE [continuing]. Shared identify—because I want to—abide by the Chairman——

Ms. SCHNECK. No. Working with——

Ms. JACKSON LEE [continuing]. Identify law-abiding citizens and is the companies have the responsibility of removing the personal data?

Ms. SCHNECK. The companies have a responsibility to make a good-faith effort. This is a policy puzzle that which is being solved each day by working together with each different equity with the private sector, with law enforcement, with the intelligence community. We are doing our best to get everybody to design that.

Ms. JACKSON LEE. Mr. Chairman, I am just gonna say this for the record and then yield back.

You all issued $25 million in cybersecurity education grants. I noticed that States to the west of the Mississippi, including Texas, have not been included. I would like to meet with whoever is appropriate to talk about these important grants. Because we need a vast array of representation. So would someone let me know who I should be meeting with?

Ms. SPAULDING. Absolutely, Congresswoman. That was announced by the Department of Energy for historically black colleges and universities. We will absolutely make sure that you get a full briefing on that and hear your thoughts.

Ms. JACKSON LEE. I thank the gentleman for his courtesy. Thank you. I yield back.

Mr. CLAWSON. The Chairman recognizes the gentleman from Texas, Mr. Hurd.

Mr. HURD. I would like to also thank y'all for being here. This is an important topic. I know a little something about it. I spent 9 years as an undercover officer in the CIA. My job was collecting intelligence on threats to the homeland. But I also did some offensive cyber operations and I recognize the dangerous threat that is out there. Helped start a cybersecurity company, as well. I have been doing that for the last 5 years. It is pretty scary, the folks that y'all have to help defend against. So it is a difficult job. But I appreciate you all being here.

My question is, you know, when you look at Border Patrol and ICE, they have difficulty sharing information amongst each other. A lot of it is structural issues; right? You know, it is—and then you talk about, you know, having DHS sharing with FBI or CIA or NSA. Even more difficult. Then also trying to do it with the private sector. I know this is one of the areas that these new entities have been created to do.

My question is, you know, in an attack of the magnitude that we are starting to see, one of the most important things that you need is you need timely information. What is the system—how are y'all trying to design this so that the information is timely?

Ms. SCHNECK. So as information comes in, it will go through a process that is automatic. So that is fractions of a second for a machine. Indicators will be available through those standard protocols that every machine can read and every machine can send. So right now, we are depending our real-time sharing on people to all be in the room to get it at once to create a report and to fan it out. Now you will have machines do it at their speed, which is the speed of the adversary.

This already works in pockets in the private sector, protecting against bot-nets. A few tens of thousands of machines light up with bad behavior, and the rest of the world can block against them. We will do that for extended threats, as well as the ability to combine what we see of protecting the Government, combining it with what we see which may be partnered or bought from private sector, and creating a large set of data that can be provided to all.

Mr. HURD. So how do you plan on sharing tactics, techniques, and procedures that the bad guys are using; right? It is one thing to have an IP address or a piece of digital code that you can share, that you can share quickly. But some of the—you know, they are looking at certain, you know, ports or the style of the attack. How is that gonna be shared with the broader community?

Ms. SCHNECK. I think two ways. One is, that is currently shared today across the agencies and with the private sector through trusted relationships. The other way is as we see those indicators coming in, we build patterns that can be combined. Again, this is where the CTIIC can help, as well. That can be combined with the intelligence they would give us and creating an even broader picture for then people to disseminate that context.

Mr. HURD. Thank you. Thank you for that. The other area is, you know, the stuff that you are talking about, obviously, the level of classification of the data, you know, is not going to be a problem because you are sharing it, you know, with folks. But how do we address the classification of threat information that is gathered by, you know, elements throughout the entire Federal Government to push that down to the private sector?

Ms. SPAULDING. So this is also an issue that we deal with on a regular basis currently. We have a couple of ways we address this. One is, as I mentioned, the enhanced cybersecurity services program that we are implementing and have implemented, where we work with managed security providers to build systems that can take Classified information and, while protecting sources and methods, use that information to provide enhanced cybersecurity solutions to their customers.

So this is a way for us to use Classified information, to protect private-sector entities, without having to clear all of those private-sector entities to receive the information. So that is one way.

The other thing that we do is we do interact on a very regular basis with the help of our intelligence and analysis I&A directorate, headed by General Frank Taylor, with the intelligence community to help them understand what is the information that we need to get out more broadly and what is the information we don't need to share that might implicate sources and methods.

That granularity we are able to achieve because we bring in cleared private-sector folks who look at the intelligence and say as a network defender, this is the piece I need. I don't need to know where it came from. I don't need to know all of these other things that are very sensitive. But this bit I need. Then we can go back to the intelligence community and say this is the piece we really need to get out to folks.

That equities review process is actually working fairly well. We have shortened the amount of time that it takes to run through that process significantly. We also have ways of, again, working to mask sources and methods and be able to disseminate that information.

So these are issues we are working through, but would love to sit down and talk with you. You might have some additional insights and ideas for us to continue to push that boundary.

Mr. HURD. Thank you. I yield back.

Chairman MCCAUL [presiding]. Thank you, Mr. Hurd.

The Chairman now recognizes my fellow co-chair of the cybersecurity caucus, Mr. Langevin.

Mr. LANGEVIN. Thank you, Mr. Chairman. I thank you, Mr. Chairman, and Ranking Member Thompson for the attention and support you have been giving to this topic for many years. In many ways, you and I were pioneers on this—in the Congress on the challenges we face in cyber space.

I want to thank our panelists for their testimony today, for the work you are doing on this issue. I applaud your work and the Department's work, and especially the President's leadership on trying to better protect the Nation's cyber space, close the glaring vulnerabilities that we face.

Of the range of things that we could do in this area and clearly, we face significant challenges, I have often said that this is never a problem, unfortunately, that we are going to solve. It is a problem to be managed. Right now, the aperture vulnerability is wide open. What we need to do is shrink this down to something that is much more manageable.

I have often said that the single most important thing we can do in closing that aperture vulnerability is information sharing. Right now in many ways we are fighting this battle with both hands tied behind our back. If we can inform, the Government can share the information that it has with private sector more easily and private sector can share the threat and the hacks that they are experiencing, we can disseminate that, we are going to be light years ahead of where we are right now.

So with that point—and maybe, Dr. Fischer, I will start with you. Information sharing is in many ways, it is a means to an end. It is undoubtedly an important means. However, as has been demonstrated, even at DHS, for example, during Heartbleed, perfect information is useless without appropriate processes, protocols, and people to act on it.

So based on your scholarship, can you give a base assessment of the proportion of cyber incidents that only suceeded because information about a known threat was not disseminated? How substantial an impact do you foresee cyber information sharing legislation, such as the President's proposal, having on the overall state of cybersecurity?

Mr. FISCHER. Well, Congressman, I would have to get back to you on the specifics with respect to what there might be—what the proportion of attacks that have been, say, prevented specifically with respect to—because of cybersecurity information sharing.

The question, though, with respect to—I mean, part of the problem here is that there are—information sharing, as a number of people have said, is no silver bullet. It is an important tool for protecting systems and their contents. As long as organizations are not implementing even basic cyber hygiene, there are going to be some significant difficulties.

So companies—there are demonstrated cases of companies that have had the information which—but nevertheless, did not pay sufficient attention to it. They have had information they could have used to prevent an attack.

If a company is not prepared to implement sort of threat assessments that they receive, then that is going to be a problem. A recent study by Hewlett Packard I think indicated like 45 percent of companies do not actually have sufficient basic cyber hygiene. So those sorts of companies are not going to be able to actually implement information sharing effectively. So—and what was the second part of your question, sir?

Mr. LANGEVIN. I wanted to know the substantial impact that you perceive that information-sharing legislation would have on the—such as the President's bill would have on the overall state of cybersecurity.

Mr. FISCHER. Right. That is something—there is a fundamental sort of issue about the effectiveness of information sharing. It is very difficult to measure—and there have been attempts by a number of folks. I saw a recent study by the Rand Corporation, for example, to try to analyze what the effectiveness of information sharing is.

So you start out with a baseline. So the question is well, what is the current baseline for information sharing? How much would actually improving information sharing improve cybersecurity? There are plenty of examples, specific examples. It is very—I think one could make a fairly compelling case on principle as to why improving information sharing is important.

But to really be able to determine its actual effectiveness will require, I think, additional information and study, and perhaps some information that is not readily available now. So I am sorry I can't give you a—you know, a definite answer to it. But it is an important challenge, and one I think that a number of people are thinking about.

Mr. LANGEVIN. Well, my time is expired. But I will have additional questions for our witnesses. I just want to thank you for the expertise you bring to the table, the work you are doing in this, and I look forward to supporting you in your efforts.

Thank you, Mr. Chairman.

Chairman MCCAUL. Thank you. Thank you for your strong interest and leadership on this issue.

The Chairman now recognizes the gentleman from Georgia, Mr. Carter.

Mr. CARTER. Thank you, Mr. Chairman. Thank you to each of you for being here.

This is obviously something that is very needed. I want to speak about small businesses, in particular. I am a small business owner, or I was. My wife is now. But, you know, I have three independent retail pharmacies, have 19 employees. This is important. This is important to my business, just as it is important to a big corporation. But it is tough. It is tough for us to adhere to some of the

37

procedures, some of the policies that we are gonna be forced to adhere to. Do you take that into account at all?

Ms. SPAULDING. We absolutely pay, as the deputy said, particular attention to small and medium-sized businesses. So the first thing that I want to point out is that even with this information-sharing legislation, it is all voluntary. So there are no new requirements being imposed on businesses of any size pursuant to this legislative proposal.

But that said, even a company that wants to voluntarily participate in this may be challenged by a lack of resources and the ability to bring on the human resources.

So we do look at how can we facilitate better cyber hygiene by small and medium-size businesses. Because they make up the important part of that cyber ecosystem in which our critical infrastructure swims. We all swim in the same ocean. As we saw in the Target breach, those small companies can be an opening for an adversary.

So I will let the deputy address a request for proposals for information that we put out to the cybersecurity solution providers to say, what ideas can you give us from your innovation in the private sector to specifically address the needs of small and medium-size businesses? Because we understand that is a real challenge, but it is critically important.

Mr. CARTER. Well, and thank you for recognizing that.

Ms. SCHNECK. So as I mentioned earlier, it is the small businesses and State and locals that also keep me at night. Two initial things I did when I came here. First is we put money to protect the State and local governments and gave them management security services that we paid for. We couldn't do that for small businesses.

So what we did was put out a request for information, which is basically asking all the companies to please tell us how would you use your innovation and use your desire for revenue, use the market to drive better, faster, safer, cheaper solutions that can enable, whether you are a small business that makes the solution, makes money off it, or whether you are one that gets the protection from it.

The other piece I want to make very, very clear is in all this technical talk, the main thing is that as we as a Government are able to put together this indicator information, that is available for you. You don't have to give us anything. So you will inevitably, as any business, buy a few widgets to protect yourself. Whatever those widgets are in our vision—and I don't mean in 5 years, I mean hopefully in 1, if not sooner—will be able to start to talk to our big database and get what we have. We are not asking you to necessarily deliberately share things. So we are trying to just make it available to you because we recognize that.

Mr. CARTER. Well, good. Thank you for that. But let me ask you, thus far have you had a good participation rate from small and medium-sized businesses?

Ms. SCHNECK. I have a binder literally that thick full of responses to that proposal and requests for information that could lead to a request for a proposal. The team is looking at how we act on that. It will go into a larger strategy in the name of efficiency in cybersecurity really across DHS with all the components, the two pieces of cyber.

But our State and local and Tribal territorial is—and our small-to-medium business work—is huge to us. This is homeland security, not big business security. It is everybody.

Mr. CARTER. Right. Right. Well, let me ask you this: Specifically to health care, do you see any specific threats in that? I mean, you know, we have insurance information. We have Social Security numbers, birth dates. I mean, we have everything that is essential that would use in a patient's information. What are the real threats there?

Ms. SCHNECK. So I think that any time you have a computer that is connected to the internet, somebody can see whatever it stores. So the adversaries are looking for whatever the motive that was mentioned earlier, they can get that information. So what you have to do, no matter what the information, is find the best way to secure those assets. We will work with you on that. We have people in each of the areas that can work with you on that and partnerships with the U.S. Chamber of Commerce to get this message out.

Ms. SPAULDING. We are absolutely seeing activity in the health care arena. Some of which appears to be for financial gain. It is a target-rich environment with very rich information; beyond just Social Security numbers or credit card numbers, for example; but information that can perpetrate other criminal schemes, such as Medicare fraud. So——

Mr. CARTER. Exactly.

Ms. SPAULDING. Right? So we are watching that very carefully. The FBI and others in law enforcement are looking at this.

Mr. CARTER. Well, great. Thank you very much for what you are doing. We appreciate this.

Mr. Speaker, I yield back.

Chairman McCAUL. Appreciate the promotion in my title. But I am not sure I would want to be Speaker right now, to be honest.

The Chairman now recognizes Mrs. Watson Coleman.

Mrs. WATSON COLEMAN. Thank you, Mr. Chairman. Thank you for the generosity you demonstrated with the information sharing that we have been doing here today.

First of all, let me just acknowledge the fact that this has been an incredible experience for me, information that you have given me today. I am really very, very proud that there are two women at this helm. I get to say that without possibly being a discrimination complaint, being a woman. But it is unusual, and it is an illustration that women should really be in these areas much more. You all are fantastic. So are you, Mr. Fischer. You are fantastic too.

But even so, I have so many questions I just don't even know where to begin.

First of all, let me ask this. There is the—this CTIIC, which is being proposed. There is the NCCIC, which exists. Thank you so—oh, NCCIC. Sure enough is. CTIIC and NCCIC.

So what is the guarantee that the new proposal, this CTIIC, doesn't wander out there and become the face of the interaction with businesses and companies and stuff and basically infringes upon the NCCIC?

Ms. SPAULDING. Congresswoman, first of all, let me echo your plug for encouragement for more women to get into STEM fields. I think it is critically important. So thank you for that.

With regard to the CTIIC and the NCCIC, the CTIIC is very clearly defined in the President's roll-out of this, which I believe occurred this morning, just a couple of hours ago. As a place for integrating the intelligence information, it is really to help Government. It is a Government-to-Government. To help the centers that exist already, including the NCCIC, to have a common operating picture and all sorts of intelligence analysis that we can provide to the private sector.

Again, we will also be taking in information from the private sector and with appropriate safeguards for privacy and civil liberty, sharing that with both the intelligence community and law enforcement as appropriate to help enrich the common picture that we all have.

So it—its responsibilities and its role are pretty clearly defined, and I think very distinct from the role of the NCCIC which, again, has been defined both by this committee and again in the President's legislative proposal as the central place for interacting with the private sector with regard to indicator information.

Mrs. WATSON COLEMAN. Should we not come up with the funding, should there not be a funding solution on the 27th of February? Will the two of you be working on the 28th?

Ms. SPAULDING. We will, Congresswoman. We will be working without a paycheck. But we are under the statutory definition. But I will tell you in my organization, the National Protection Programs Directorate, which is responsible for critical infrastructure security and resilience, we will be down to 57 percent of our workforce.

Mrs. WATSON COLEMAN. Are you at full force right now?

Ms. SPAULDING. Right now we are at full force. But of our a little over 3,000 employees, if there is a funding hiatus, we will be down to 1,748. So it will be, again, 57 percent. I want to point out that those numbers include—most of those numbers are the Federal Protective Service, which engages on a daily basis in the critical mission of protecting Federal facilities, and our office of biometrics and identity management, which uses biometrics to particularly keep known and suspected terrorists out of the country.

Mrs. WATSON COLEMAN. That is pretty scary.

Ms. SPAULDING. Two critical important missions, they will be on the job. But the rest of my workforce that worries about critical infrastructure in the private sector, cyber, will be down to about 9 percent—normal strength——

Mrs. WATSON COLEMAN. So I have two quick questions, because that is pretty scary. I need to know the difference between ISAOs and ISACs.

Ms. SPAULDING. Yes.

Mrs. WATSON COLEMAN. My other questions is to Mr. Fischer real fast. What is it that this new proposal that the White House has put out, what does it address that is deficient in what exists now? Did we need to do this in an entirely new legislative approach, or could there have been some tweaking to what already existed? Thank you.

Ms. SPAULDING. So I should point out under the—in a funding hiatus, our—again, we are gonna make sure that we have in place everything we need to have in place to protect lives and property on a daily basis. So our NCCIC will continue to function. But the analytic support that feeds that and helps prioritize those activities will be hampered, and the roll-out of the things that I mentioned earlier will be hampered.

The ISAC, ISAO—ISACs information and analysis centers are a kind of information sharing and analysis organization. So they are a subset, ISACs share a subset of ISAOs. What the administration's Executive Order hopes to do is to encourage additional coming together of private-sector entities to share information.

Mrs. WATSON COLEMAN. Thank you. Mr. Fischer.

Mr. FISCHER. So what the—there are, I should preface by saying that there are some observers who would argue that, in fact, new legislation is not really necessary; that current mechanisms are sufficient. But there are plenty of people who actually think the opposite, as well.

With respect to what the new legislation would do, the White House proposal, it would create some mechanisms, including the establishment of these ISAOs for the receiving and sharing of information that don't really exist now, or that exists in another form; like, for example, the ISACs exist now but they are—the ISAOs are somewhat different from that. It specifically designates the NCCIC as a particular role with respect to receiving and sharing this kind of information.

It also would provide certain—it tries to remove these barriers that have been mentioned that private-sector organizations may have for sharing information and make sure to—and provide protections for things like privacy and——

Mrs. WATSON COLEMAN. So you said, I believe, that there is both the issue of barriers, and there is the issue of incentives; incentives perhaps doing something, eliminating or minimizing some of the barriers. So is the incentive just simply the value of the sharing of the information, or is there some other kind of incentive that needs to use to encourage these businesses to engage in this?

Mr. FISCHER. Right. So, I mean, one of the questions is what would the—why would a company want to share information? One way, of course, to encourage them to share information is to reduce the risks to them of sharing that information. But at the same time, what are they going to get out of sharing it? Are they doing it as simply a—something that they think is for the public good, or are they gonna get something back?

So one of the ways that they might get something back is through reciprocity. So, for example, if they are a member of an ISAC or perhaps an ISAO, they may have some relationship with that organization that ensures that if they provide information, they will be able to get information.

But of course, with respect to the Federal Government, there have been enough concerns about, you know, forcing organizations to give information to the Federal Government that, in fact, all of the legislative proposals say that they are voluntary.

Mrs. WATSON COLEMAN. Thank you, Mr. Chairman. I yield back.

Chairman McCAUL. The Chairman now recognizes the Chairman of the Subcommittee on Cybersecurity, Infrastructure Protection, and Security Technologies, Mr. Ratcliffe.

Mr. RATCLIFFE. Thank you, Mr. Chairman.

Ms. Spaulding, I would like to start with you. The administration's proposal discusses how Federal agencies—and I will quote— "through an open and competitive process will choose a private entity to identify and develop a common set of best practices for the creation and operation of private information sharing and analysis organizations."

The NIST, the National Institute of Standards and Technology led a collaborative process last year to develop the cybersecurity framework. Why isn't this NIST framework, why isn't it being utilized in the process here?

Ms. SPAULDING. Congressman, I think it will be utilized in the process here. What the NIST framework does is provide a framework, a way for companies to think about their cybersecurity and how to achieve better cybersecurity. So it breaks it down into five key functions; identify, identify the assets you want to protect and the risks that it faces, ways to protect, ways to detect, ways to respond, and ways to recover. It pulled together from the private sector their best practices in each of those categories. So that is the cybersecurity framework.

What this standards organization will do is to look at what are the best practices for these ISAOs. Of the ISACs, of the ISAOs, of the information-sharing organizations that are out there today, which are the best ones, what are the best practices that we see out there? Let's pull that together as a guideline for private-sector groups that want to come together to say here are some of the best practices in terms of ways in which they are protecting the information that has been given—that is being shared in there. So that I know that if I give it to you, you are only going to share it within this ISAC, for example. Or ways in which you are going to protect privacy information, et cetera; ways in which you are gonna get it out quickly to me, get back to me, so that I get information for information I give in. How do I know I am going to get something good back from it?

So it is a different set of best practices. But the process for developing that will be very similar to the one NIST used. This third-party standards organization, will be canvassing the private sector, the existing public and private-sector sharing organizations to say to them tell us what you think are the best practices. Very collaborative is what we envision.

Mr. RATCLIFFE. Sure. So I want to talk a little bit about this— a single portal for information sharing. As a former terrorism prosecutor after 9/11, while we would have liked the information to come through one single avenue, what was more important was that people would share information. So whether it was with the FBI or whether it was with Secret Service, we encouraged information sharing.

So I am wondering if you can expound on the process here, the thought process behind there just being one single portal for sharing information.

Ms. SPAULDING. Yes, absolutely. We totally agree. The highest priority is on information sharing. Again, that is such a high priority, that even if it is only sharing between private-sector companies and they don't share with the Government, we think that is worth promoting, because sharing of information is gonna significantly advance the ball here.

But with respect to sharing with the Government, again, we want to make sure that existing relationships are not disrupted here. So companies that have relationships with the FBI, with Treasury, with other parts of the Government and are comfortable picking up the phone and calling them, they should continue to reach out and say we think we see something, you know, that looks a little strange on our system; we think we may have some intrusion activity here. That kind of information sharing across Government we hope will continue to take place.

What we are trying to do—and even sharing of cyber threat indicators can be shared—you know, we are not saying you can't share it with other departments and agencies.

We are creating a newly-incentivized program. If we are doing that, we want to use that to help us create a common operating picture. So rather than have that information coming in in a distributed, dispersed way all across the Government and hope that it comes together somewhere at some point, sometime, we want to say we would really like to incentivize you to bring it in to this one place, and we will take responsibility for making sure that it gets to the people who need it very quickly.

But this way, we are—greater confidence, both that we have a common operating picture and that privacy protections are clearly in place.

Mr. RATCLIFFE. Terrific. Thank you, Ms. Spaulding.

Very quickly, Dr. Schneck, I wanted to give you an opportunity. Ms. Spaulding and Dr. Fischer were able to expand on Congresswoman Watson Coleman's question about privacy.

Just very quickly, I want to give you an opportunity. Can you explain the processes in which NCCIC protects privacy and explain that relationship with DHS privacy office?

Ms. SCHNECK. So thank you. Very quickly, DHS has one of the first statutory privacy officers. We work not only with the front office at that level, but the under secretary has for our directorate her own privacy officer that reports up. Every program that we have engages them. When I came in I actually asked—because I write code. Or I used to—the people that write code, I asked them; are you getting rid of the extra memory so that there isn't—because this is one of the famous ways that attackers attack—so that there isn't a gap that we didn't know about that is actually storing information that we didn't know about.

Every step of the way in how we build our programs, we work with those teams on privacy. We also do impact assessments, which means a document is published on our website. What we do, what we collect, what we are doing with it, and why we do it. As we grow these capabilities, that is an ingrained philosophy in who we do at DHS.

There has never been a harder time to want companies, as we heard before and it is true, to share with Government. There has also never been a more urgent time to put the indicators together to respond to an adversary that candidly has an infinite appropriation and does whatever they want.

We need to make sure that we have our defensive capabilities as strong as they are. That means putting this data together. It is speed and privacy and the balance therein. It takes all hands on deck, everybody to work this. Part of the reason it is taking us more than just a few months to build this capability is because we have to build it with the right privacy, the right policy, and the right equities to make it light speed and get it right. Does that answer your question?

Mr. RATCLIFFE. It does. Thank you. I am out of time. But I do want to thank you all of you for being here and for better informing the committee Members so that we can hopefully move forward with cyber legislation in this Congress. I yield back.

Chairman MCCAUL. Thank the gentleman. Excuse me.

The Chairman now recognizes Mrs. Torres.

Mrs. TORRES. Thank you, Mr. Chairman. and I also want to join my colleagues in thanking the panel—or the witnesses for being here. Most of all, for spending an entire hour with some of us, ensuring that we understand and that we somehow feel at peace that you are collecting data that is absolutely necessary, but actually being very cautious at ensuring that individual privacy rights are being abided by.

We have also heard a lot from the perspective of corporate America. But what I haven't heard yet coming from you is how you plan to communicate everything that you are doing with the general public. So someone like myself at home, where my computer gets hacked and my IP address gets duplicated 15 times, how is my information as an individual victim or survivor of a hack attack in my personal network, how are you going to protect me from sharing my personal information with anyone else?

I haven't heard it from a perspective that I think the general public can relate to. We have been speaking at this level, and we haven't really simplified it in a way that my constituents could be comfortable with what we are doing here.

So could you explain a little bit as to—in the private session, you know, we heard specific information of what would be pulled. Can you speak to that here?

Ms. SPAULDING. Congresswoman, thank you for the question. As I hear it, it involves at least two aspects. One is as a private citizen, what does this mean to me; right? How is what you have just been describing here for the last couple of hours relevant to protecting my identity information——

Mrs. TORRES. Right.

Ms. SPAULDING [continuing]. For example, my PII?

What I would say to that is that by protecting the networks and systems that hold your information, we are protecting you—and your—against identity theft, for example. One of the pieces of legislation that the administration proposed—we have talked about their information-sharing legislation, but they also proposed breach notification legislation. That is very much designed to protect consumers; to make sure that companies have a single standard across the country for being required to notify individuals when there is reasonable basis to believe that their personal information may have been stolen, and to do so promptly. So that is very much geared toward the individual and the consumer.

In terms of how do we reassure them that this work that we are doing on their behalf is not interfering with their privacy interests? As we have talked today, we are very much focused on the specific information that we need to defend networks. We are very precise. The legislation the administration has proposed defines that information very carefully.

The automation that we are building will have a structured way of providing that information that will minimize the likelihood that information we don't need could be included. We place a very high priority on making sure that we are—we have no interest, it does not help our network defense to gather a lot of personal information about Americans or others.

I will let the deputy address that, as well.

Ms. SCHNECK. I would only add that it is my hope that we can use campaigns like our "Stop. Think. Connect." messaging or the awareness that we do every October in cybersecurity awareness month. I think every month should be cyber awareness month. But we focus that month to get out on the road and talk to everyone.

I am hoping that the public will start to understand this. We have to work to take some of our technical terms and make them actually English. But start to understand that Government is working very hard to protect them. It starts with getting our own agencies talking, which we are doing. It starts with building into the private sector. Then making sure that through its providers of theirs of other programs with agencies in the Federal Government that work directly with citizens, that we get that right. But we need to really enhance the trust relationship in the cyber area.

Mrs. TORRES. So I am almost out of time. I just want to make sure that I get my two other questions answered.

To this issue though, my final word on this is that we need to ensure that that community outreach is part of whatever legislation that we can produce; that community grants and opportunities to include the public in this discussion happens.

Mr. Fischer, the fair information practice principles we have been talking about, mentioned in the President's—in his security Executive Order, how are they incorporated into the Department procedures, from your perspective?

Mr. FISCHER. Well, I think the Department people would probably be better-situated to answer the specifics with respect to that. But I think on the question of how privacy is incorporated, it is a—one of the difficulties—and this also gets back to your earlier question a little bit—that the general public has various views of what privacy means. There isn't any one really universal kind of understanding. I mean, there is something called, you know, "personally identifiable information," which is kind of interpreted as being something that, you know, could actually identify a person specifically.

But when people think about privacy, they don't necessarily think about it in the same way as Government may think about privacy. So, you know, if one is going to develop a set of principles or use a set of principles or, in fact, incorporate something like pri-

45

vacy by design, which has been around for a long time, or something that people have tried to do, it is—there—it can become very complicated very quickly.

I think one of the things that is very important is to be able to create a way of letting people understand specifically what the issues are so that there can become really a consensus among consumers about what it is that we are really trying to protect.

Because one more point here, which is, you know, people are always worried about—understandably, about Government and its role. But, in fact, people willingly give huge amounts of information to private companies.

Mrs. TORRES. We do.

Mr. FISCHER. If you get software that is free, it just means you are the product. Because the company is getting something out of it. Usually, that means they are getting information from you; right?

Well, people don't even often realize this. You know, the service agreements that we sign, I mean, who has time to read through them or can understand them? So I think it is very important that there be a—you know, a dialogue, really, about how to characterize privacy more clearly for everybody so there can be consensus.

Mrs. TORRES. Thank you. I think I am out of time. I yield back.

Chairman MCCAUL. Recognize the Ranking Member for closing comments.

Mrs. WATSON COLEMAN. Thank you. I just want to thank the entire panel for giving us this time today and the information. Particularly, I want to thank you, Honorable, Honorable, Honorable Spaulding and Dr. Schneck, because you have given us the majority of the day when I knew you could be doing some other things, including preparing for what might be a furlough of some very important people. I hope you don't have to do that. But I want you to know and I thank you, Chairman, for guiding me through this very moment of being next to you. Thank you.

Chairman MCCAUL. Well, you did quite well, I must say.

Let me thank the witnesses. Let me thank Ms. Spaulding and Dr. Schneck for your service to our country on a very important issue. I think the education process is very important for Members of Congress and for the American people to identify that this is a real and valid threat that we need to defend the Nation from. The hearing will be open for 10 days, the record I should say.

Without objection, the committee stands adjourned.

[Whereupon, at 1:51 p.m., the committee was adjourned.]

APPENDIX

QUESTIONS FROM RANKING MEMBER BENNIE G. THOMPSON FOR SUZANNE E.
SPAULDING AND PHYLLIS SCHNECK

Question 1. According to the testimony of the under secretary, the White House legislative proposal on information sharing would immunize against civil or criminal liability entities that voluntarily disclose to or receive lawfully obtained cyber threat indicators from the NCCIC or a private ISAO that has adopted certain best practices. Please explain the scope of the liability protection, including a delineation of the circumstances in which liability protections would not be afforded to an entity that chooses to disclose or receive information from the NCCIC or a certified ISAO.

Answer. The President's information-sharing legislative proposal provides targeted liability protection to private entities that voluntarily disclose or receive lawfully obtained cyber threat indicators from a private information security and analysis organization (ISAO) or the National Cybersecurity and Communications Integration Center (NCCIC). It affords such entities protection from public disclosure, and from use of disclosed indicators as evidence in a regulatory enforcement action.

The proposal directs DHS to select a non-governmental Standards Organization for the purpose of identifying a common set of best practices for the creation and operation of private ISAOs. The Standards Organization will work directly with the public to identify and develop best practices. To receive the liability protection afforded by the President's proposal, private-sector entities must share with the NCCIC or an ISAO that has self-certified that it adheres to these best practices.

Question 2a. To receive liability protection, does a private entity need any kind of certification from the NCCIC or an ISAO to which it disclosed or from which it received cyber threat indicators?

If so, what standards would guide an NCCIC or ISAO in issuing such a certification?

Answer. There is no NCCIC- or ISAO-issued certification. The proposal directs DHS to select a non-governmental Standards Organization for the purpose of identifying a common set of best practices for the creation and operation of private ISAOs. The Standards Organization will work directly with the private sector to identify and develop best practices. To receive the liability protection afforded by the President's proposal, private-sector entities must share with the NCCIC or an ISAO that has self-certified that it adheres to these best practices.

The proposed independent standards organization for ISAOs would not promulgate Government-determined standards or require a compliance certification. It would be an independent organization that sets forth voluntary standards that it will develop in consultation with the public.

Question 2b. If no certification were required or issued, would a court in the first instance have to assess whether a private entity deserves immunity under Section 106?

Answer. ISAOs would have to self-certify under Section 106 of the information-sharing proposal. That self-certification is distinct from any acknowledgement of receipt that the NCCIC or the ISAO might generate as a way to reassure an entity sharing threat indicators that it has submitted the information to the correct place.

Question 3. What are the limitations of the ISAC model that necessitate the effort to increase the proliferation of ISAOs?

Answer. An ISAC is a type of ISAO. In practice, as ISACs have evolved, they are sector-specific entities that encourage information sharing within specific critical infrastructure sectors. While ISACs have had a great deal of success and lessons learned that will serve ISAOs as they form, many companies do not fall within a designated sector or fall within multiple sectors. And some companies want to share with partners outside of their sector for a wider scope of situational awareness.

Encouraging ISAOs beyond just ISACS will provide for more organizational flexibility. ISAOs can be organized around a particular region, community of interest,

48

or concern about a particular type of cybersecurity risk. ISAOs could include companies regardless of their sector affiliation.

Question 4. What are the risks and rewards of an information-sharing environment that is dominated by ISAOs?

Answer. Critical infrastructure includes both physical and cyber infrastructure, publicly- and privately-owned. The ISAO model builds upon the successes of existing models. The formulation of ISAOs allows and encourages organizations to participate in cyber threat information sharing to proactively detect and prevent cybersecurity incidents before they can cause damage to their networks by applying the knowledge, capabilities, and experiences of a wider community. Sharing cyber threat information broadly and with sufficient timeliness can improve the Nation's cybersecurity writ large by reducing our cyber adversaries' advantages of speed and stealth.

QUESTIONS FROM HONORABLE JIM LANGEVIN FOR SUZANNE E. SPAULDING AND PHYLLIS SCHNECK

Question 1. In reviewing the President's information-sharing proposal, I was drawn to the phrase "lawfully obtained" as it relates to cyber threat indicators. Due to ambiguities in anti-hacking statutes, courts have not yet settled whether the work of many well-intentioned security researchers—so-called white-hat hackers—is lawfully obtained. How can we work to ensure that information-sharing legislation does not chill vital security research while at the same time not opening the door to companies "hacking back"?

Answer. The President's information-sharing proposal aims to emphasize that activities conducted to obtain cyber indicators should comply with the law. The Department of Justice is best positioned to answer questions pertaining to the relevant statutes and to what extent they apply to the activities of cybersecurity researchers.

Question 2. It is vitally important that we incent private-to-private information sharing, something the President's proposal does through the use of Information Sharing and Analysis Organizations (ISAOs). However, ISAOs need only self-certify to be able to receive threat indicators. Without any independent oversight to be sure that best practices are being followed, are you concerned that this could lead to a reduction in privacy?

Answer. Having publically-available standards for ISAOs, including standards for privacy protection, will help ISAO member companies hold their ISAO accountable. ISAOs that are transparent and accountable are likely to attract more members, providing an incentive to clearly demonstrate compliance with the standards.

Question 3. We know that cyber threat information is most valuable when shared expeditiously, which, in this domain, essentially means at machine speed. How can DHS lead efforts to ensure that the stripping of PII is accomplished as thoroughly and quickly as possible so that the information shared is timely?

Answer. DHS requests that, before sharing cyber threat information with the Department, partners filter out any PII, content, and other information that is not necessary to describing the cyber threat. In addition, currently, DHS Analysts are required to review cyber threat indicator information for PII and handle it as outlined in US–CERT standard operating procedures. Generally, DHS's policy is to minimize or redact any personal information that is not necessary to understand or analyze a threat. As we move to automated threat indicator sharing, DHS and interagency partners are studying privacy-by-design technical safeguards as well as policy and process approaches to minimization that include a combination of automated removal and/or filtering of sensitive data, oversight capabilities, and where necessary, manual review. Technical safeguard requirements may also be required. To safeguard Americans' personal privacy, the administration's cybersecurity legislative proposal requires private entities to comply with certain privacy restrictions, such as removing unnecessary personal information and taking measures to protect any personal information that must be shared, in order to qualify for liability protection. The proposal further requires the Attorney General, in coordination with the Secretary of Homeland Security and in consultation with the Privacy and Civil Liberties Oversight Board and others, to develop receipt, retention, use, and disclosure guidelines for the Federal Government.

Any future cybersecurity legislation will incorporate strong privacy, confidentiality, and civil liberties safeguards while strengthening our critical infrastructure's security and resilience DHS is committed to furthering information sharing and promoting cybersecurity standards for critical infrastructure.

QUESTION FROM RANKING MEMBER BENNIE G. THOMPSON FOR ERIC A. FISCHER

Question. What are the risks and rewards of an information-sharing environment that is dominated by ISAOs?

Answer.[1] This question cannot be answered definitively at present. Such an answer would depend on several factors that are currently unknown or uncertain. However, the analysis below may be useful in helping to determine the potential benefits and disadvantages of the ISAO model in such an environment.

ISAOs (Information Sharing and Analysis Organizations) are defined in the Homeland Security Act (6 U.S.C. § 131(5)) as "any formal or informal entity or collaboration created or employed by public or private sector organizations" created to assist in securing critical infrastructure and protected systems by acquiring, analyzing, or sharing "critical infrastructure information," which refers to non-public information relating to threats to and defense and recovery of critical infrastructure or protected systems.

Information Sharing and Analysis Centers (ISACs) are more familiar to most observers. They may also be considered ISAOs but have a different origin, having been initially formed pursuant to a 1998 Presidential directive (PPD 63) on critical infrastructure protection.[2] The directive called for a single ISAC but also for a National Infrastructure Protection Center (somewhat analogous to the National Cybersecurity and Communications Integration Center [NCCIC]) that would "establish its own relations directly with others in the private sector and with any information sharing and analysis entity that the private sector may create."[3] Also, the directive stated that the "actual design and functions" of the ISAC would "be determined by the private sector, in consultation with and with assistance from the Federal Government." The result was the creation of several sector-focused ISACs, rather than a single entity. Many of today's ISACs are associated with Federally-recognized critical infrastructure sectors. Eighteen are listed as members of the National Council of ISACs (NCI).[4] There are currently 16 Federally-recognized critical infrastructure sectors.[5] The table below shows the relationships between those sectors and the ISACs.

Critical Infrastructure Sector	Information Sharing and Analysis Center
Chemical	
Commercial Facilities	Real Estate ISAC
Communications	Communications ISAC (National Coordinating Center for Communications–NCC)
Critical Manufacturing	
Dams	
Defense Industrial Base	DIB–ISAC
Emergency Services	EMR–ISAC
Energy	ES–ISAC (electric sector) Oil and Gas ISAC
Financial Services	Financial Services ISAC
Food and Agriculture	
Government Facilities	Multi-State ISAC
Healthcare and Public Health	Health ISAC
Information Technology	IT–ISAC
Nuclear Reactors, Materials, and Waste	Nuclear Energy Institute
Transportation Systems	Aviation ISAC Maritime ISAC Public Transit ISAC Surface Transportation ISAC
Water and Wastewater Systems	Water ISAC
No specific critical-infrastructure sector	Research and Education ISAC Supply-Chain ISAC ICS–ISAC (industrial control systems)

Source.—See text.

---

[1] Some responses were prepared in consultation with other CRS experts.

[2] The White House, "Presidential Decision Directive 63: Critical Infrastructure Protection," May 22, 1998, *http://www.fas.org/irp/offdocs/pdd/pdd-63.htm.*

[3] It is not clear what "others in the private sector" refers to, as the NIPC was a Federal entity. Presumably, this was a drafting error.

[4] National Council of ISACs, "Member ISACs," 2015, *http://www.isaccouncil.org/memberisacs.html.*

[5] The White House, "Critical Infrastructure Security and Resilience," Presidential Policy Directive 21, (February 12, 2013), *http://www.whitehouse.gov/the-press-office/2013/02/12/presidential-policy-directive-critical-infrastructure-security-and-resil.*

Notes.—A Food and Agriculture ISAC and a Chemical ISAC were established in 2002 (Government Accountability Office, *Critical Infrastructure Protection: Improving Information Sharing with Infrastructure Sectors,* July 2004, *http://www.gao.gov/assets/250/243318.pdf*) but appear to be no longer operational. The NCC, within DHS, has served as the Communications ISAC since 2000 (*http://www.dhs.gov/national-coordinating-center-communications*). The ICS–ISAC is not listed as a member of the NCI. Other entities such as State governments may also have ISACs.

As the table shows, ISACs currently exist for 12 of the designated critical infrastructure sectors.[6] There are also three ISACs that are cross-sectoral. There appear to be few organizations that call themselves ISAOs at present.[7] The concept increased in prominence following a legislative proposal and an Executive Order from the Obama administration in January and February of 2015 fostering their development and use.[8] The White House described the intent as "expand[ing] information sharing by encouraging the formation of communities that share information across a region or in response to a specific emerging cyber threat. An ISAO could be a not-for-profit community, a membership organization, or a single company facilitating sharing among its customers or partners." The Executive Order specifies that "ISAOs may be organized on the basis of sector, sub-sector, region, or any other affinity," that members may be public sector, private sector, or both, and that an ISAO may be "a not-for-profit community, a membership organization, or a single company facilitating sharing among its customers or partners."[9] Under the proposed legislation, ISAOs that wish to protect members from liability risks for sharing information would need to be self-certified according to standards to be developed under a process to be established by DHS.

If this approach were adopted by Congress, ISAOs could possibly become dominant entities in the information-sharing environment. Given the uncertainties associated with their anticipated impacts, it may be best to examine possible effects through a series of questions:

- *Would ISAOs lead to more information sharing among private-sector entities and between the NCCIC and the private sector?* The broad and flexible nature of the ISAOs envisioned in the administration proposal, as opposed to ISACs as currently configured, could lead to the creation of ISAOs for affinity groups for which ISACs are not viewed as applicable—for example, the entertainment industry, with companies such as Sony.[10] That could lead to much broader information sharing among private-sector entities that join the ISAOs and with the NCCIC. Yet, there is no guarantee that new ISAOs would be established, or, if they were, that they would lead to increased information sharing either among the members or with the NCCIC. Even for a few CI sectors, some former ISACs are no longer in operation, and the degree to which existing ISACs are active in information sharing is considered variable by many observers. Furthermore, the degree to which the NCCIC could process and usefully disseminate the volume and variety of information it may likely receive from a large number of ISAOs is uncertain.

- *Would increases in information sharing through ISAOs improve cybersecurity?* The relationship between the volume of information shared and improved cybersecurity is not straightforward. Both providers and recipients—whether they are businesses, ISAOs, or Government agencies—will incur various costs, in-

---

[6] Some caution should be exercised with respect to the completeness of this list, as there may also be organizations that have ISAC-like functions but do not call themselves ISACs.

[7] One example is the HITRUST Alliance (see Testimony of HITRUST Alliance CEO Dan Nutkis, *Cybersecurity: The Evolving Nature of Cyber Threats Facing the Private Sector,* 2015, *http://oversight.house.gov/wp-content/uploads/2015/03/3-18-2015-IT-Hearing-on-Cybersecurity-Nutkis-HITRUST.pdf*). Some organizations may function like ISAOs or ISACs but not call themselves that.

[8] The White House, *Updated Information Sharing Legislative Proposal,* 2015, *http://www.whitehouse.gov/sites/default/files/omb/legislative/letters/updated-information-sharing-legislative-proposal.pdf*; The White House, "Fact Sheet: Executive Order Promoting Private Sector Cybersecurity Information Sharing," Press Release, (February 12, 2015), *http://www.whitehouse.gov/the-press-office/2015/02/12/fact-sheet-executive-order-promoting-private-sector-cybersecurity-inform*; Executive Order 13691, "Promoting Private Sector Cybersecurity Information Sharing," *Federal Register* 80, no. 34 (February 20, 2015): 9349–53, *http://www.gpo.gov/fdsys/pkg/FR-2015-02-20/pdf/2015-03714.pdf.*

[9] The Homeland Security Act definition is both broader, in that ISAOs can be "any formal or informal entity or collaboration created or employed by public or private sector organizations", and narrower, in that under the act, the organizations must be "created or employed" for "gathering and analyzing," "communicating or disclosing," and "voluntarily disseminating" critical infrastructure information as specified in the act (6 U.S.C. 131(5)). The administration proposal does not appear to limit ISAOs to information about critical infrastructure, although its focus is on cybersecurity, rather than on the all-hazards emphasis in the act.

[10] However, the IT–ISAC already lists Sony as a member (*https://www.it-isac.org/*).

51

cluding developing, assessing, processing, sharing, and applying the information. For sharing to be effective, information from the provider must be relevant to recipients' needs and in forms that can be readily applied in their IT and security environments. Recipients must also have the capacity and willingness to assess and use the information received in a timely fashion. A large increase in the amount of information received may in fact be counterproductive, especially if much of the information proves to be of little use to the recipient. In theory, ISAOs can be closely tailored to the needs of their members and therefore help ensure that those needs are met. However, a closely-tailored ISAO might not provide information relevant to all the lines of business in which members may engage, and membership in several organizations might be preferred.[11]

- *Would ISAOs provide overlapping or duplicative services?* One potential advantage of the sector-focused approach taken by the ISACs is that it can minimize such duplication. However, it can also create gaps for entities that do not fall clearly into one or another ISAC sector or that are multi-sectoral. Addressing such gaps is one of the stated purposes of the administration's ISAO proposal. In addition, the potential for duplication creates the potential for market competition, and such market forces would ideally yield more innovation and more rapid improvement in information sharing than would a more restricted approach. Market forces might also lead to lower costs, and cost is often cited as an impediment to improved information sharing, especially for small businesses. Yet market forces might also lead to higher costs, and a proliferation of ISAOs might also make decisions about which one or ones to join more difficult for potential members. It also creates the possibility that members could receive conflicting information or even recommendations from different ISAOs. At present, there appear to be few examples of potentially overlapping information-sharing entities. One possible case is in the health sector, which has both the Health ISAC[12] and an ISAO, the HITRUST Alliance.[13] Services provided by the two appear to be both complementary and potentially competitive.[14]

- *Would for-profit ISAOs be beneficial or disadvantageous for improving information sharing?* The administration proposal states that for-profit entities that share information can be ISAOs. That would presumably include internet and cybersecurity service providers, for example. Such entities might be particularly well-positioned to share information efficiently and effectively with customers and to bring market forces to bear favorably in the information-sharing environment. However, unintended adverse impacts are also possible. For example, for-profit companies might have a resource and marketing advantage over non-profit organizations, and some may perceive such an advantage as unfair or counterproductive. It is also possible that competitive pressures may impede information sharing involving more than one company. Some entities that could potentially be ISAOs are currently members of ISACs and could also be members of other ISAOs, creating possible conflicts of interest.

- *Would a cybersecurity environment dominated by ISAOs complement or encumber improvement of cybersecurity risk management?* The NIST Cybersecurity Framework,[15] developed to assist critical-infrastructure and other entities in adopting effective cybersecurity risk management, discusses the role of information sharing in cybersecurity, including the roles played by ISACs and other entities in helping organizations determine their desired levels—called tiers—of cybersecurity implementation. Each of the four tiers includes descriptions of risk-management processes and programs, and "external participation," which largely describes the level of information sharing in which the organization engages.[16] Broad availability of involvement with ISAOs could help organizations

---

[11] For example, Sony is involved in electronics, gaming, movies, and music. However, it is not clear whether Sony would have been better protected against recent attacks against it if it had been a member of ISAOs in any of those subsectors in addition to its membership in the IT-ISAC.

[12] National Health Information Sharing and Analysis Center, "NH–ISAC," 2015.

[13] Nutkis, *Testimony at COGR Hearing*.

[14] See, for example, Marianne Kolbasuk McGee, "NH–ISAC Offers Cyber-Intelligence Tool," *Data Breach Today*, December 5, 2014, *http://www.databreachtoday.com/nh-isac-offers-cyber-intelligence-tool-a-7642*.

[15] National Institute of Standards and Technology, *Framework for Improving Critical Infrastructure Cybersecurity*, Version 1.0, February 12, 2014, *http://www.nist.gov/cyberframework/upload/cybersecurity-framework-021214-final.pdf*.

[16] A Tier-2 organization "knows its role in the larger ecosystem, but has not formalized its capabilities to interact and share information externally," whereas a Tier-4 organization

Continued

that so desire to move to higher tiers with respect to information sharing. However, as the Framework makes clear, that is only one facet of cybersecurity implementation. There may be a risk, therefore, that a proliferation of ISAOs would lead to an overemphasis on information sharing to the detriment of other, possibly more critical cybersecurity needs, thereby resulting paradoxically in a decline in overall cybersecurity preparedness.

- *Would the proposed ISAO standards process sufficiently address concerns such as those raised above?* Both the legislative proposal and the Executive Order call for designation of a nongovernmental organization whose purpose would be to specify a "common set" of "best practices" or "voluntary standards or guidelines" for creating and operating ISAOs. Such standards and practices may help address some but not all of the issues discussed above. For example, standards may be helpful in determining what kinds of information may be most useful to share for different purposes and different kinds of entities, as well as how best to use such information, but it seems unlikely that they can address concerns about overlapping or duplicative services, or problems such as gaps in coverage for key groups caused by economic factors.

If ISAOs do in fact proliferate, it is very likely that substantial changes will occur in the information-sharing environment, but many of those effects may be difficult or even impossible to predict accurately. However, there appear to be few independent assessments of the performance and effectiveness of current information-sharing entities and their relationships.[17] Some studies have concluded that measuring the effectiveness of information sharing is difficult in the current environment,[18] and the creation of a large number of ISAOs could further complicate any assessments. Such concerns might be addressed by options such as on-going independent research and evaluation activities designed to determine the effectiveness of ISAOs, perhaps as a part of or complementary to the standards-development and revision process envisioned by the administration. That could potentially be started in conjunction with another option-staged implementation of the ISAO model, perhaps including pilot programs.[19]

QUESTIONS FROM HONORABLE JIM LANGEVIN FOR ERIC A. FISCHER

Question 1. In reviewing the President's information-sharing proposal, I was drawn to the phrase "lawfully obtained" as it relates to cyber threat indicators. Due to ambiguities in anti-hacking statutes, courts have not yet settled whether the work of many well-intentioned security researchers—so-called white-hat hackers—is lawfully obtained. How can we work to ensure that information-sharing legislation does not chill vital security research while at the same time not opening the door to companies "hacking back"?

Answer. The current cybersecurity environment creates a number of dilemmas, and one of them is captured by this question. The problem is that the complexities of cyberspace—whether hardware, software, networks, or the people using them—combined with its rapid technological evolution and the changing threat environment, create significant challenges for distinguishing appropriate and inappropriate behavior, especially by those pursuing protective and defensive activities. Such ambiguity can create problems for legal and ethical interpretation of such actions and is believed by at least some observers to have a potentially chilling effect on needed research. This is not a new issue,[20] but some legislative proposals to improve cybersecurity have led to increased attention to the concern.[21]

" . . . actively shares information with partners to ensure that accurate, current information is being distributed and consumed to improve cybersecurity before a cybersecurity event occurs (ibid., 10, 11).

[17] One example is Government Accountability Office, *Public Transit Security Information Sharing: DHS Could Improve Information Sharing Through Streamlining and Increased Outreach*, September 2010, *http://www.gao.gov/assets/310/309903.pdf*.

[18] See, for example, Matthew H. Fleming, Eric Goldstein, and John K. Roman, *Evaluating the Impact of Cybersecurity Information Sharing on Cyber Incidents and Their Consequences* (Homeland Security Studies and Analysis Institute, March 31, 2014), *http://papers.ssrn.com/sol3/papers.cfm?abstract_id=?2418357*; Brian A. Jackson, "How Do We Know What Information Sharing Is Really Worth?," Product Page, (2014), *http://www.rand.org/pubs/research_reports/RR380.html*.

[19] These options are provided for purposes of illustration. CRS does not make recommendations or take positions on legislative issues.

[20] Aaron J. Burstein, "Conducting Cybersecurity Research Legally and Ethically," April 4, 2008, *https://www.usenix.org/legacy/event/leet08/tech/full_papers/burstein/burstein_html/index.html*.

[21] See, for example, Jan Ellis, "Will the President's Cybersecurity Proposal Make Us More Secure?," *Security Street*, January 23, 2015, *https://community.rapid7.com/community/infosec/*

In addition, researchers who are part of an established and recognized enterprise, such as a university or research institution, are likely to have different opportunities and constraints than those who operate independently, without either the benefits or the strictures of an institutional environment. Also, *research* may refer to many different activities, from the acquisition of fundamental knowledge about threats, vulnerabilities, and defenses, to the development of hardware, software, and procedures to address cybersecurity needs, to the investigation of specific incidents for purposes of attribution and response. Constraints on research are likely to apply to such different classes of researchers and activities in significantly different ways.

One of the core challenges in finding ways to reduce the risk that the legal environment will chill needed research is in reaching a clear consensus among stakeholders about what constitutes proper and improper research activity. If such a consensus can be reached, legal ambiguities might be much more easily resolved. Without a consensus, resolution is likely to be very difficult. For example, some may argue that a research exception should be provided in communications privacy laws,[22] but without agreement on what is and is not appropriate behavior, such an exception may be difficult to scope.

Another issue that may be worth considering is lack of understanding and education among researchers about what they can and cannot do under current law and regulations. Researchers may be reluctant to take some actions that are lawful solely because of uncertainty about their legality.[23] One way to address this issue is to provide researchers with access to appropriate education resources that can clarify what is permitted and also provide guidance for reducing the risk of violating legal requirements.[24] For example, the legal risks associated with the use of honeypots—websites or other information resources specifically designed to attract attacks—may depend, some have argued, on how they are implemented.[25]

Finally, an option available for some research problems is the use of isolated testbeds or "cyber ranges." Such facilities are designed for research and training, can mimic many features of cyberspace, and permit a wide range of actions that could possibly be illegal if done in "the wild." However, they are limited in scale and may otherwise be unable to mimic the environment of cyberspace sufficiently for some kinds of research. In addition, if they are not completely isolated from the internet, the risk of impacts on external systems would need to be considered.

Question 2. I think I can safely speak for everyone on this panel in saying that we agree that cyber threat information sharing is important. I believe that the President's proposal will help lower legal barriers to information sharing. What are other obstacles that could continue to keep information sharing from being as ubiquitous as we'd like?

Answer. Awareness of the potential utility of information sharing in cybersecurity appears to be increasing. As the question points out, legal barriers are only one set of obstacles that would need to be overcome for ubiquitous and effective use of this cybersecurity tool. Several additional potential obstacles are discussed below.[26]

Resources

The costs of information sharing vary, but may be prohibitive for some entities. The costs of obtaining information from an entity such as an ISAC may be comparatively low,[27] but that is only for a mechanism to receive information. The information must be processed by the recipient and applied where appropriate. That will require staff time and perhaps additional hardware and software, especially for implementation of so-called "real-time" information sharing, which often involves machine-to-machine communication and action. Such costs may be particularly problematic for small businesses, which may be of concern not only because of their broad role in the economy, but also because the sector includes many innovators

---

blog/2015/01/23/will-the-president-s-cybersecurity-proposal-make-us-more-secure; Mark Jaycox and Lee Tien, "Obama's Computer Security Solution Is a Mishmash of Old, Outdated Policy Solutions," January 16, 2015, *https://www.eff.org/deeplinks/2015/01/obamas-computer-security-solution-mish-mash-old-outdated-policy-solutions*.

[22] Burstein, "Conducting Cybersecurity Research."

[23] Ibid.

[24] See, for example, Jody R. Westby, *Legal Guide to Cybersecurity Research* (Chicago, IL: American Bar Association, Section of Science & Technology Law, 2013).

[25] Burstein, "Conducting Cybersecurity Research."

[26] The list is not intended to be definitive or exhaustive. That would require a comprehensive, objective study of all aspects of information sharing in the broader cybersecurity context. In addition, any such list is likely to change significantly as cyber space and its component threat and information-sharing environments continue to evolve. The items in this list are not presented in any order of priority or desirability.

[27] See, for example, N. Eric Weiss, *Legislation to Facilitate Cybersecurity Information Sharing: Economic Analysis*, CRS Report R43821.

54

that can be inviting targets for cyber espionage, and because many are contractors with larger organizations that may be inviting targets for cyber crime.[28]

Awareness

Concerns about the lack of awareness about cybersecurity in general and information sharing in particular, especially within the private sector, have been longstanding. While the NIST Cybersecurity Framework[29] and other efforts, along with media attention to major breaches, appear to have resulted in some increased awareness of the need for better cybersecurity, it is not yet clear the degree to which awareness has improved as a result. Awareness of a problem or need is also not sufficient on its own. To be effective, it must be translated into appropriate action, which often may not be the case. For example, according to a 2012 survey, three-quarters of small businesses believe that cybersecurity is important, but only 10% have a written policy on it.[30]

Usefulness of Information

Many kinds of information can be shared, from threat intelligence[31] to business strategies and best practices. In addition, the same information may have different utility for different users—for example, threat signatures relating to attacks on one critical infrastructure sector may be of marginal concern for another, and best practices may be much more useful for small businesses than signatures associated with advanced targeted threats. Also, shared information may prove of little use if it is delayed, provided without relevant contextual detail, or provided in a form that requires substantial additional processing to determine its applicability. If recipients find that the information they are provided is of little use to them, they may be less likely to participate in or continue with information-sharing initiatives.

Application of Information

Information sharing by itself is not sufficient to improve cybersecurity. Not only must it be actionable—presented in a form that can be usefully applied—but the recipient must also have processes, including equipment and software, in place to use the information effectively. If such processes are not in place and utilized properly, the net effect is the same as if the information were not shared at all.[32]

Reliability of Sources

There are several reasons why sources of information may not be considered reliable by potential recipients. For example, the source may be a competitor, such as another business. The kinds of information the source provides may focus on a set of entities other than the one to which the recipient belongs. Or the source might have a reputation for providing erroneous, outdated, or otherwise useless information. If no sources are available to an entity that it deems reliable, it may be reluctant to participate in information-sharing activities.

Mechanisms for Information Sharing

Currently, there appear to be two general models for information sharing—a decentralized, "peer-to-peer," often informal approach between entities with complementary needs, and a more centralized "hub-and-spoke" model such as the ISACs.[33] Organizations such as ISACs are generally sector-specific. Not all sectors have such organizations, and other affiliations other than sector may also be important for some kinds of information sharing. Filling such gaps appears to be part of

---

[28] In the attack on Target, the criminals accessed the store's computer system through a compromised system of an HVAC contractor (see N. Eric Weiss and Rena S. Miller, *The Target and Other Financial Data Breaches: Frequently Asked Questions*, CRS Report R43496).

[29] National Institute of Standards and Technology, "Cybersecurity Framework," August 26, 2014, *http://www.nist.gov/cyberframework/index.cfm*.

[30] About a quarter have an "informal" policy (National Cyber Security Alliance, Symantec, and JZ Analytics, 2012 *NCSA/Symantec National Small Business Study*, October 2012, *https://www.staysafeonline.org/ . . . /2012_ncsa_symantec_small_business_study.pdf*).

[31] This can be described as "indicators (i.e., an artifact or observable that suggests that an attack is imminent, that an attack is underway, or that a compromise may have already occurred); the TTPs [tactics, techniques and procedures] of an adversary; and recommended actions to counter an attack" Chris Johnson, Lee Badger, and David Waltermire, *Guide to Cyber Threat Information Sharing (Draft)*, SP 800–150 [National Institute of Standards and Technology, October 2014], 4, *http://csrc.nist.gov/publications/drafts/800-15sp800_150_draft.pdf*.

[32] See, for example, Johnson, Badger, and Waltermire, *Guide to Cyber Threat Information Sharing (Draft)*.

[33] Denise E. Zheng and James A. Lewis, *Cyber Threat Information Sharing: Recommendations for Congress and the Administration* (CSIS, March 2015), *https://csis.org/files/publication/150310_cyberthreatinfosharing.pdf*.

55

the rationale behind the administration's ISAO proposal.[34] On the one hand, the absence of an appropriate mechanism can be a barrier to information sharing for an entity. On the other hand, a proliferation of mechanisms, such as some observers fear the administration's ISAO model might result in, could also serve as a barrier if it makes information sharing inefficient or confusing for possible participants.

Standards

The adoption of standards for information sharing is one way to help address concerns about reliability and utility of information received. Dozens of standards exist relating to information sharing.[35] The Department of Homeland Security has been developing a single set applicable to sharing of threat intelligence.[36] Lack of a broadly-accepted set of consensus standards or a framework for information sharing might impede more wide-spread adoption of information-sharing activities.

Economic Incentives

Some observers have noted that the benefits of receiving cybersecurity information tend to outweigh the benefits of providing such information for many organizations.[37] In addition to legal issues that may be associated with providing information, businesses may be concerned about reputation costs, if they provide information showing that they have been victims of cyber attacks. In the absence of incentives for reciprocity, it is hard to see what benefit an organization would gain from providing information, unless it is a Government entity whose mission is to provide such data or a provider of cybersecurity services. Government measures such as requirements for data-breach notification, as enacted in most States, can provide incentives for organizations to share information about attacks that may be used to help prevent future attacks on other entities or to capture and prosecute cyber criminals.

Reducing the Need for Information Sharing

Some observers have expressed concern about risks associated with an overemphasis on the role of information sharing in cybersecurity. It is only one of many cybersecurity tools. For example, it is a relatively small part of the NIST Cybersecurity Framework, and target levels of sharing vary among the tiers the Framework identified.[38] In addition, information sharing tends to focus on immediate concerns such as cyber attacks and imminent threats. While those must be addressed, that does not diminish the need to reduce risks through design and implementation of more secure systems and networks—sometimes referred to as "building security in"—and finding ways to change the incentive structure within cyber space to increase the costs and reduce the potential for profit from cyber crime and activities of other adversaries.

○

[34] The White House, *Updated Information Sharing Legislative Proposal*; The White House, "Fact Sheet: Executive Order Promoting Private Sector Cybersecurity Information Sharing"; Executive Order 13691, "Promoting Private Sector Cybersecurity Information Sharing."

[35] European Union Agency for Network and Information Security, *Standards and Tools for Exchange and Processing of Actionable Information*, November 2014, https://www.enisa.europa.eu/activities/cert/support/actionable-information/standards-and-tools-for-exchange-and-processing-of-actionable-information.

[36] Department of Homeland Security, "Information Sharing Specifications for Cybersecurity," 2015, https://www.us-cert.gov/Information-Sharing-Specifications-Cybersecurity.

[37] See, for example, N. Eric Weiss, *Legislation to Facilitate Cybersecurity Information Sharing: Economic Analysis*, CRS Report R43821; Zheng and Lewis, *Cyber Threat Information Sharing: Recommendations for Congress and the Administration*.

[38] National Institute of Standards and Technology, *Framework for Improving Critical Infrastructure Cybersecurity*, Version 1.0.